confessions of a slacker mom

confessions of a slacker mom

Muffy Mead-Ferro

Da Capo

LIFE
LONG

A Member of the
Perseus Books Group

Cataloging-in-Publication data for this book is available from
the Library of Congress.

First Da Capo Lifelong Books edition 2004
Originally published by Pince-Nez Press. Reissued by
arrangement with the author.
ISBN 0-7382-0994-5

Published by Da Capo Lifelong Books
A Member of the Perseus Books Group
http://www.dacapopress.com

Da Capo Lifelong books are available at special discounts
for bulk purchases in the U.S. by corporations, institutions,
and other organizations. For more information, please
contact the Special Markets Department at the Perseus
Books Group, 11 Cambridge Center, Cambridge, MA 02142,
or call (800) 255-1514 or (617) 252-5298, or e-mail
special.markets@perseusbooks.com.

2 3 4 5 6 7 8 9-08 07 06 05 04

For my mother

TABLE OF CONTENTS

chapter 1

Good-bye, herd

-1-

For us moms or moms-to-be in these information-awash and overachieving times, it feels as though, somehow, we've become everyone else's property. Wards of the state. Imbeciles.

We can't put a toe out of bed in the morning without feeling the pressure to buy a bunch of expensive equipment and do a whole load of nutty and, frankly, inconvenient things in the interest of being a supermom and producing a superkid. We're inundated with instructions on how best to achieve these goals. And we're not supposed to question either one – the instructions or the goals.

It makes me want to put my toe right back under the covers and keep it there.

About halfway through my pregnancy with my daughter Belle, I began to balk. By then I was well acquainted with the graphic testimonials and detailed advice that this physical state invariably elicits from people. But I started to take exception to all the guidance I was getting.

An early indication that I might end up a slacker mom was a tendency toward sarcasm. "Like I need a smart baby," I muttered, when hearing about the latest device for stimulating her intellect in-vitro.

This negative attitude was accompanied by recurring fits of laziness. "When pigs fly," I thought, as I evaluated the odds of my carving out time to engage in such dreary activities as charting her fluid intake and bowel movements.

These disquieting and politically incorrect feelings increased in frequency and intensity throughout my pregnancy. Yes, kind of like labor pains. I did my best to ignore them, however. I hadn't really started to see myself as a slacker, much less feel good about the idea.

Just the opposite, in fact. While spending 60 hours a week in a love-hate relationship with the largest client at the advertising agency where I worked, I was dutifully taking all my prenatal vitamins. I'd quit smoking crack altogether. Actually, I never smoked crack, but I was made to feel that dry martinis and double lattes amounted to the same thing, so I quit drinking both of them.

I was also reading all five of my pregnancy-advice books simultaneously. And, I was trying to keep up with all the expert guidance I was getting from magazines, TV shows, websites and complete strangers standing next to me in the department store aisle. I was pregnant – the chips were down.

I was never even sure what that phrase refers to, but to me it conveyed the paranoia I felt. " The chips are down," I kept reminding myself.

In other words, do not screw up now, because there's no turning back.

But I was already feeling inadequate. For instance, I could not find the time to sit around with headphones stretched over my abdomen playing Mozart to my fetus in an effort to make her better at her multiplication tables.

I had seen the tummy-headphone outfits in catalogs, along with the proof of their effectiveness. Well, not proof, exactly, but lots of glowing testimonials from non-slacker moms whose objectivity was somehow never in doubt. I didn't buy them though, and my task-oriented personality was making me feel guilty.

From what the product description promised, these contraptions stood at least some chance of turning my kid into a real egghead. So how could I justify not buying them? How could I let day after irreplaceable day of my pregnancy go by as my fetus, the little slacker, just loafed the time away in my dull, unstimulating womb?

They're expensive? I'm busy? Feeble excuses, considering what was apparently at stake.

But it was all I could do just to hold down a job, keep appointments with my hair stylist, and try and get the nursery put together. Those last two weren't easy, either. My responsibilities to my clients involved weekly travel. I didn't have a lot of time at home, much less in baby supply stores.

I did eventually set aside a Saturday for a marathon baby-apparatus shopping spree with the help of a super-organized girl-friend. She'd had her first baby eight months before, so from my standpoint she knew just scads about child-rearing. Looking back, I realize (as I'm sure she does) that she was as addled as I was. A victim of all the same marketing campaigns and societal pressure that every other new mom is subjected to.

That day, I was right there with her. She'd generously prepared a four-page list of mission-critical items for me to purchase in a mad race from one end of the city to another. I didn't even question it. I was in that to-hell-with-the-budget frame of mind that it's so easy to get into when you're deranged. Or eight months pregnant.

I spent that entire day, contributing more than my share to the national epidemic of credit card debt. But I only knocked 90 percent of the items off my list, and it was that last tenth that was, illogically, making me feel I was further behind every minute.

In particular, I had yet to receive the bassinet I'd ordered weeks and weeks before from one of the more snooty baby stores, and really didn't know what I would do if that bassinet did not arrive before D-day. My baby needed a place to sleep, for God's sake! I didn't know whether to call the store and continue to hassle them, or just sneak over there with a can of gas and torch the place.

I was a ticking time bomb, basically. Above the neck as well as below.

Thankfully, the evening after that exhausting and expensive day of shopping, I happened to get a phone call from a friend in Alaska. Mother of two, with a third on the way. She had called to check on how my late-in-life pregnancy was going, and to inquire about my career plans following the birth of my baby.

When she asked if I was ready to have this new little person in my life, I was too fixated on the slapdash condition of my nursery to know that she was probably talking about my emotional readiness, not my equipment list. So I told her that I was not even close to being ready because I still required a number of crucial items. Namely, the bassinet.

Her response to this desperate state of affairs was to loudly guffaw. "Are you kidding?" she said. "My little boy slept in a crab crate his first six months."

That silenced me for a speck. I knew I'd heard her right. She said "crab crate." One of those cage-type deals made of nailed-together wooden slats that's been underwater, with crabs in it. Eww. I did feel sorry for the little boy.

That waste of sympathy came and went pretty quickly how-ever. Her little boy didn't care. If he didn't care, why should she? And apparently she wasn't concerned about what other people thought either. That was the most startling and impressive of all. If a mom could get away with this in Alaska . . . right away I saw where this could lead me.

When I got off the phone, I went into the bathroom, looked at the stressed-out woman in the mirror and asked her pointblank, "Are you daft?"

I didn't even recognize myself. I'd grown up on a cattle ranch, for cripes sake. In our family, we were supposed to tell the cows where to go, not join the herd! And I didn't need someone in Alaska telling me how to rough it – I was the daughter of Mary Mead – a woman who stuck us in a mud puddle to play when my brothers and I were little.

My mom did things her own way. She never had a bassinet and she probably never did any of the things I had on my To-Do list. Maybe I wasn't ready to throw that list in the garbage. But I was ready to take a good, hard look at it.

By then I'd changed my mind about the overdue bassinet. In fact, I probably would have called and canceled my order if I hadn't already indicated to the store manager that it was a matter of life and death. There were lots of other places my baby could sleep. A cardboard box was a suite at the Plaza for all she'd know.

I thought as well about the other nursery provisions I'd spent so much money on that day, and I regarded them with a new skepticism. Looking at them objectively for a change, there were a few of them I could still categorize as essentials (thermometer), but more of them would now have to be classified as luxuries (changing table). And to be completely honest with myself, quite a few of them would best be described as a big pile of plastic debris (infant activity center).

I also considered the strains of Mozart's Piano Concerto No. 21 which I wasn't piping into my womb. "My mom never did that," I said to myself, "and I was always pretty good at math." When it occurred to me that Einstein's mom didn't do it either, I went right ahead and crossed that off my list of things to feel guilty about.

My enlightenment never did lead to my newborn sleeping in a cardboard box, though, because the European bassinet I'd been so concerned with arrived in time. At least it was attractive – it wasn't made of yellow plastic. I put it in the same category as Prada loafers, an extravagant personal indulgence. This made me feel a little better about its price tag.

I have no problem with extravagant personal indulgences, by the way. I just want to call them by their real name. And be clear about whether I'm indulging myself or my kid.

The bassinet was a case of me indulging me. It did serve a purpose, too, for about three months. But not an essential purpose. And by then I knew that if anything here was essential, it was that I start thinking for myself.

Of course, thinking for yourself is not exactly easy when you're in that state of pre-baby delivery that seems to dictate an all-out spending binge, decorating rampage, and whirlwind of dusting and vacuuming, right up until your water breaks. I guess this condition goes by the rather congenial term of "nest-building." But, in cases like mine, the term "prenatal lunacy" was probably more apt.

Some of that must be unavoidable, especially if it's your first baby. But I've discovered that being creative and improvising not only saves me a lot of time and money, it's also setting an example that might actually be useful to my children.

The example of making-do.

If you don't know what I mean by "making-do," just ask your grandmother, if you're lucky enough to still have one. Making-do is a way of accomplishing amazing things such as baking up an apple pie with no apples.

My grandmother married into a Wyoming cattle ranching family, and if she didn't know how to make-do before then, she must've learned right away. She tells how it was to raise her little boy and girl (my uncle and my mom) on the ranch in the '30s and '40s. They could only make the five-mile trip into town two or three times during the long, deep winters. And when they did go, it was on a sleigh wagon pulled by two draft horses. Not a quick trip.

Even if she'd lived in town, the local market wouldn't have stocked powdered formula, disposable diapers, prepared baby food, or any of the other things I took for granted, and probably couldn't have gotten along without. They didn't even have apples ten months of the year.

"How did you do it?" I've asked her several times.

"I just did," she always says.

"But how?" I persist. She had none of the proper equipment or instructions by today's standards. But she never describes motherhood as a hardship.

My grandmother wouldn't look down on contemporary moms, though. She would say it's just practical to take advantage of modern conveniences if you've got access to them. But it illustrates the relative nature of "need" when you consider that previous generations have raised lots of happy and healthy babies – even smart ones – without any of the things I had on my baby shopping list.

Listening to my grandmother's recollections has given me a stark perspective on what is – and what is not – an essential baby supply. I thought of her when I opened a baby shower gift that turned out to be one of those gadgets known as wipe-warmers. I'm talking about a little plug-in container that keeps wipes warm, so baby's bottom doesn't feel any change in temperature during a diaper change, for those of you who live in outer Mongolia and don't already know this.

My grandmother still remembers getting her homemade, hand-washed cloth diapers off the clothesline in the cold Wyoming winter.

"It was like bringing in a stack of boards," she says.

Not that they went from there to the baby's bottom. They became warm and pliable enough after hanging all day over a line strung behind the wood stove in her living room.

My mom was also a making-do virtuoso. I suppose she learned that from her mother. Or maybe life on a remote Wyoming cattle ranch dictates that. So might life in a fishing village or a garment district or a mining town. I'm sure most moms of a generation back were better at making-do than we are today. So my family's not unique in that respect.

One way we differed from most American families, though, is that we didn't have television. We tried like mad to get it, and experimented with many dubious reception methods involving tinfoil. But we never could get TV until cable came along, and they finally ran one out to the ranch. By then I was in my teens.

Thanks to that technology gap, I missed out on a huge body of cultural knowledge in which all my friends are conversant. They can all sing the Brady Bunch theme song and the Oscar Meyer jingle. I doubt you were spared those influences the way

I was. So you already know what it took me 20 years working in advertising to fully appreciate.

You know that if you've got television, you've got somebody incessantly telling you, over and over, without reprieve (yes, I'm being redundant – just emphasizing one of the most important ways we all know marketing works) that you've got to have a certain brand of, say, diapers. It's hard not to be convinced when they show you the droves of babies who've achieved total satis- faction from these diapers. Even if you realize deep down that these babies are, in fact, professional actors.

Even more cunning is when the commercials dramatize your deepest fears in a scenario where the bungling incompetence of the mom is revealed to the world as her baby shows up in a competing brand of diaper, leaking on the mother-in-law's blouse.

By this time, you know on a subconscious level, at least, that you must either be mentally deficient or grossly negligent if you choose not to purchase their product.

Why do advertisers think this kind of guilt-driven message will work with moms? I don't see them speaking this way to fathers, I really don't. Are we mothers that insecure? Is that how we get talked into such harebrained things as abdomen-phones?

I don't know. But I do know what will happen if I buy into

all those marketing messages and actually purchase all the kid gear I see touted in parenting magazines or attractively displayed in stores. The first thing that will happen is I'll be bankrupt. But the second thing is I'll be depriving my children of that invaluable life-lesson, taught by example, of making-do.

My mom learned it from my grandmother and I want my kids to learn it from me. Maybe that way, when they grow up, they'll be more resourceful. Which might even get them further ahead than being super-smart.

Whenever I feel like I'm getting caught up in the modern neurosis that seems to accompany child-rearing, I just ask myself, what if I'd had my babies in an isolated Alaskan fishing village and didn't have access to the breast-feeding counselors or toddler-fitness classes? Or what if I were raising my children back on the ranch during the depression and simply couldn't afford all the educational toys and extracurricular activity fees? Would it mean that my kids were automatically disadvantaged, wouldn't have skills, and wouldn't achieve success in life?

The answer's always "No, no, and no." In fact, I'm more and more convinced that our kids may be quite a bit better off when they don't have all the so-called advantages.

As I've thought about how to raise my kids, I've thought a

lot about how my mom and dad raised me. My mom died before I had my daughter Belle and my son Joe, but my memories of her parenting style have inspired me every day. She was truly a slacker mom, in the loveliest and most agreeable sense of the word.

It's not that I think the way my parents raised my brothers and me is what everyone else should do. On the contrary, I'm sure all parents have their own family stories and gut instincts.

In fact, I think parents probably have better instincts than they know. You don't have to be a pediatrician or a child psychologist or an academician to have some inborn wisdom about raising your child. You just have to be a mom or a dad with a sense of what's practical, and a willingness to listen to your inner voice, instead of bowing to the inevitable pressures of "perfect parenting" messages.

And don't think this book is just one more installment in those endless parenting archives. I'm not going to end each chapter with reference material such as, "The Thirteen Baby Supplies You Really Need" or "The Only Six Toys You Ever Have to Buy" or "The Three Disciplinary Methods That Actually Work." I'm way too much of a slacker to come up with lists like that.

But I do hope it'll give you enough to mull over that the next time you hear from some magazine, TV show, friend, or in-law about the latest thing that you, as a parent, are supposed to do or buy, you'll pause. And if you hear your inner voice saying something like "yuck," you'll listen. That's a good sign it's something you can skip, and you and your children might all be better off.

By the way, I just read an online article that says piping any kind of music into your womb actually disrupts the natural body rhythms your unborn child is supposed to be listening to.

Mmm-hmm. Just as I suspected. ⟿

chapter 2

Toys aren't us

–2–

When you find out you're pregnant, one thing you should do right away is buy stock in the parent company of Duracell.

That way, you'll be able to see how you're benefiting from the deluge of new toys you'll be getting over the next 18 years, whether you buy them or other people buy them for you. Maybe if someone had told me that, I wouldn't have my bad attitude about toys – and battery-operated toys in particular.

Maybe I wouldn't even be so irritated by all the toy marketing trying to pass itself off as cinema, as education, and as food and drink. What was Clifford the Big Red Dog originally, anyway? A book? A cereal? A television show? A stuffed animal? Does anyone remember?

Now it might sound like I'm veering off into anti-capitalist political statements, but this book is a confession. So I confess, I don't like a lot of toys. I don't enjoy picking up toys. I don't think it's fun to replace their batteries. And I really hate sorting through endless pieces of multipart toys trying to match them back up with their brethren.

In fact, while I'm confessing, let me say to those dear friends who've given Belle toys containing dozens of components that the toys came in the front door and went out the back. I decided she doesn't need something comprised of 60-plus pieces until she gets her own set of flatware.

The poor girl has never had much in the way of toys compared to her friends, no matter what the number of pieces.

I remember when we invited another family with their year-old baby boy, same age as our daughter, to my grandparents' ranch one spring weekend. They arrived with their large SUV packed window-to-window, thanks almost entirely to the one-year-old's paraphernalia.

Compared to them, we had zilch. Car seat and diaper bag. Not because we were just so disciplined or on some kind of higher plane as parents. It was partly because we owned a smaller car. But big car or not, my husband and I simply aren't interested in packing up a lot of stuff. We're too lazy, for one thing.

We did contemplate bringing a few pieces of equipment, such as the high chair. And I admit it is easier to feed a year-old baby when she's strapped in a high chair with an attached tray than when she's balanced on your lap.

But it would have meant cleaning the high chair off. Folding it up. Taking up space in our car that we'd reserved for the dogs. And then following the same tiresome routine on the way home. Yawn.

A high chair was hauled out of our friends' car, however, along with a portable crib, a stack of monogrammed blankets, and a bouncy seat. The heaviest item, though, was an oversized duffle bag full of toys. It took both fathers to lug it inside the cabin.

"Holy mackerel!" was my first thought. But then I felt guilty, and ill-prepared as a newish mom, noting all the trouble they'd taken to make sure their little boy was occupied and entertained for the whole weekend.

"I hope they won't mind sharing those," I also thought, but didn't say out loud.

I was probably aware that this made me a moocher on top of being a slacker. They often do go hand-in-hand, I realize that. But I was honestly worried because our daughter hadn't one thing to play with. We'd brought along a grand total of zero toys and activities for her. I can't even say I'd thought about it and then consciously rejected the idea. I was such a loser mom.

Fortunately, to our friends, their toys were our toys, so we were more than covered.

I was underestimating her, though, when I'd thought Belle wouldn't have had anything else to play with that spring weekend. Because during the summer that followed, we took lots of trips to the ranch without hauling a bunch of toys from home. Belle made toys out of things that were already there.

She picked up a dry willow stick discarded in the kindling pile after some long-gone marshmallow roast, and went around beating it on various objects outside the house. Just think about it – you can see how that might be fun. Bang-bang-bang, thunkety-thunk, tink, bddddddt.

Another exciting thrill was toddling back and forth across the rickety footbridge we have at the creek, getting splashed by the swelling spring runoff. (Plenty of adults have been thrilled by that crossing.) And she instantly picked up on the fun of throwing rocks in the pond.

21

Why it is that watching a rock plunk into the water, even if it's only inches from the shore, is such first-rate fun, I don't know. But it seems to be inordinately appealing to people of all ages.

Even when she had to play inside, I remember the amusement Belle got from an empty paper towel roll. She'd hoot into one end and hear her voice thrown out the other. She'd look through it and focus on a special little scene in the faraway circle. She'd drag it along the cane backs of the dining room chairs and make what to her was music. We never did break the news to her that the empty paper towel roll was not a toy.

Wait. Maybe it was a toy. Sounds like a moneymaker, too. Note to self: Call patent attorney.

But even if we'd packed and brought every "real" toy Belle owned, it wouldn't have filled up our friends' duffle bag. Thanks to my husband's tightfisted rule when it comes to toys.

I accidentally facilitated his rule when I bought a wheeled wicker basket for her little stuffed animals before she was born. It's maybe 18 inches or two feet long, and about the same height. I thought it would be a good place to stash the little bears and bunnies she got as shower gifts.

But my husband viewed it from the beginning as "her toy box." Meaning, this is it. This is where Belle will keep all her toys.

At first I tried to clear up what I thought must have been a misunderstanding. I'd meant the basket for a certain kind of toy, not all toys. It was more of a decorating scheme than a storage scheme, I explained to him with an air of magnanimous patience.

But he wasn't interested in the nursery decor. So I told him he was simply unreasonable. You could fill up the basket with just ten or twelve medium-size toys. Talk about anti-capitalist! He didn't budge, though, and has enforced the rule that if she gets more toys than can fit in this basket, we get rid of some.

Not only has he persisted in this austere approach to toy-limitation, he extended the concept and included our son Joe, once he came along. I've sneaked in a few extras by making them shelf-decorations or dress-up items that hang in the closet, but the rule has mostly been followed.

Since then, my husband has conceded that setting the toy limit where he did was completely arbitrary. And I've conceded that it would have been arbitrary no matter where we'd set it. So why not set it where it suited us? Or were we going to leave the drawing of that line to our children?

Without even considering whether the one-basket limit is good or bad for our kids, I can tell you it is lovely for us parents. It'll probably save us thousands of dollars. Hundreds of them on batteries alone.

It's not only about money, though. It's about what I've already admitted is my tendency to be slothful when it comes to monotonous chores. I didn't have my first baby until I was 38, so in addition to being inherently lazy I don't have nearly the energy a 25-year-old does. But I don't feel sorry about the fact that I don't do my share of buying, assembling, picking up, sorting, or fixing toys.

23

I'm not simply trying to avoid a mess in my kids' rooms, though. I'm also thinking about the mess I don't want in their heads. I'm pretty sure if my children were continually supplied with every latest toy, that they would quickly develop a dependence on always having something new. Where the only good toy is a new toy.

I can only imagine the consequences if they never grow out of that. Actually, I don't think I have to imagine them. I think I've seen them for myself.

I know more than one gal with the expensive habit of always having to have new clothes. I'm distantly related to someone who thinks his new car is no good after a year. And I also know of an unhappy person who intermittently feels he needs a new spouse. Perhaps, just perhaps, this all started when they were little and had an endless incoming stream of new toys.

It would be easy to get to a point in your life where you didn't value what you had at all. In fact you'd barely notice it because you'd be so intensely focused on what you didn't have. And on what you really wanted – whatever was still at the store.

Some kids who have a whole lot of toys don't seem to think much of any of their toys. It's not hard to figure out why they don't take care of them either. I'm not saying they're bad kids or even ungrateful. It's just that there always seems to be an inverse relationship between quantity and value. So the more toys a kid has, the fewer of them remain interesting. It's no big deal if parts get lost or toys are broken. There are so many others strewn around the room or languishing in the bottom of the toy box to choose from. If for some reason we can't just go back to the store for more.

But another reason kids sometimes don't value their possessions is the simple fact that they don't have to fork over the money for them.

Of course, now you probably think you're going to hear some improbable story about how, back when I was a kid and we got tired of playing with dirt clods picked up out of the corral, we had to buy our own toys.

Well, we didn't. Not all the time. But some of the time, we did.

I was about seven years old, for instance, when the hula-hoop craze made its way into my rural corner of the world in Wyoming. Benson's Hardware was the only store in town that sold toys. They got in a good supply of hula-hoops to begin with, but they were going fast. Reportedly, all my friends had one within a week of their arrival at the store.

I knew my mom wasn't planning to run into town and buy one for me, though. If we got new toys, it was nearly always because there was some specific toy-giving occasion – our birthday or Christmas.

My strict-constructionist mother didn't count a hula-hoop craze as a holiday, so I'd have to earn the money myself.

I asked her how much they cost. "A dollar and a half," she said. She also volunteered a list of jobs I could do if I wanted to earn the money. Taking out all the trash: five cents. Cleaning the bathroom: ten cents. And so on. My mother was not influenced by such radical ideas as minimum wage.

Well, over the course of just a few days I earned the money, intent on not being left out of the hula-hoop frenzy. I asked my mom if I could go with her on her next trip to town. She knew my aim and was happy to comply, but she pointed out that I only had fifty cents to spend.

I didn't understand – I thought she'd told me I needed a dollar and a half. Wasn't that fifty cents?

"No," she explained, "fifty cents is half a dollar, not a dollar and a half."

Drat. I'd been illiterate as to monetary nomenclature. I was far short, and by the time I earned all the money I needed,

Benson's would probably be out of hula-hoops.

"Oh, well," my mother said, "let's go to Benson's and see if they have any left."

It was unlike her to bail me out like that, so I'll never forget it. When we got to Benson's I hurried past the first-floor irrigation boots, hack saws, and nail bins and up to the toy department. I found that they still had one hula-hoop left, and I could see why. It was drab harvest gold, and defective, because for some reason it didn't have the beads inside to produce the swishing sound as it circled your waist. But I dismissed that as functionally insignificant, and I paid my fifty cents while my mom made up the difference.

She knew my mistake about the money was an honest one, and she never wanted me to pay back the dollar I owed her. The flawed hula-hoop became one of my most prized possessions, and I kept it long after all my friends had grown out of hula-hooping.

I remember the day I finally let it go.

"This," said my mother, "goes in the giveaway pile."

"But it's still good," I protested, meaning I still had the hang of it.

My mother frowned. "You won't have space for it in your dorm room."

I realized she was right; I was on my way to college and

should part with it. But for me, it remains an icon of a great toy. It was more than worth the money. It didn't require batteries. It didn't have a bunch of pieces. And it was so much more durable than a dirt clod.

Whether my parents paid or I paid, I never did have all the toys that my in-town playmates seemed to get automatically. We could suggest what we wanted for our birthdays and Christmas but we had to be damn picky about what we asked for. Because the opportunity wouldn't come again for a dog's age.

So, did I really have to have a new, say, Twist 'N Turn Barbie? If that's what I said in my letter to Santa, I'd probably get one. But I'd better think on it. I already had a Barbie. Was the Twist 'N Turn feature one that would make Barbie all that much more fun? Enough to justify making that my choice? Or would it for the most part duplicate a toy I already had and, frankly, was getting a little tired of?

Maybe I'd be smarter to hold out for a guitar.

Besides, I had been devising a plan for turning my rigid-waisted Barbie into a twisty-turny one. All I had to do was get my dad to put her on the table saw and cut her in half, right at the apex of her bizarrely narrow waist. Then I would have him clamp her onto the drill press and put quarter-inch holes in her

upper and lower torso, into which I could insert a greased bolt
that my father would have dutifully sawed the head off.

Barbie bodies were solid in those days, and I still think this
would have worked.

I don't know, maybe this scheme had more to do with the
fact that I *was* getting tired of Barbie. But at least I'd been born
and bred to make-do.

I also benefited, by going through this lengthy thought
process, from having my gratification delayed. Which is so
much more satisfying than when it's instant.

Of course, instant gratification is as short-lived for parents as
it is for kids. It's such a deflating experience to buy a toy for your
child because he saw it on the shelf and is just dying to have it
and he pleads and begs, and you finally take pity on him and buy
it, and then he doesn't even care about it after the first day or
even the first hour.

"Hey," I'll protest, "What happened? You said you *loved* this
toy! Did you trick me?"

I'm easily tricked, so that may well be what my children are
doing. But even if they're innocently losing interest in the new
toy, it feels so very unjust. To avoid that frustration, I try to make
sure that choosing the best toy means they have to really think it

through, over a period of time. And compare the toy in question to all the other options, just as I had to do with the Barbie versus the guitar.

In my parents' case, their ultra-conservatism about toys really had little to do with toys. It was more that whatever extra money they had went to buying land or cattle. It's not so easy to have that kind of discipline if you do have the money to buy most of the toys your kids want. And we can hardly control the toy-buying others do for us.

Some people like to shower their grandchildren with toys with a lack of restraint they never would have shown with their own children. Are they doing it to drive us into mental institutions or just because they really want to make our kids happy every minute? Who knows? But it's another reason my husband and I don't buy a toy for our kids just because they're dying to have it.

At some point, Belle and Joe will probably be dying to have every toy ever made. I say, let them put it on their wish list for the grandparents. Or carry out enough garbage to earn the money themselves.

It's not just their quantity that bothers me about toys, though. It's their features.

Today's toys, especially the educational ones, are technologically superior to the toys I grew up with. One thing this usually means is that they don't work without batteries. It also seems to mean they do more.

Have you ever noticed, though, that when a toy does more, the kid playing with it usually does less?

Wow, this violin plays music all by itself! Hey, this book reads the words for me! Gosh, this paper magically doesn't let you color outside the lines! I really wonder if this is good. It might be unthinkably bad. It might be turning our children into dimwits, dolts, and dullards. Not geniuses.

31

I can't help but think of one-year-old Belle, making a telescope, a musical instrument, and a megaphone out of a paper towel roll. Is that because she was some kind of prodigy? Or just deprived of real toys?

Of course, I like to think that it's both. But either way, that kind of inventive play has got to be more mentally stimulating than the educational toys I'm familiar with.

I don't suppose, especially with the more advanced toys, that my child is learning any skill beyond how to make that particular toy function. What is learned playing Game Boy other than how to play Game Boy?

That's not the kind of skill I want my children to be soaking up in these fleeting formative years. I'd rather they learn creative thinking. That will allow them to entertain themselves and solve their own problems. And maybe even exit childhood with some of the tools they'll need to be independent adults who are responsible for their own success and happiness.

Not that I can get Belle or Joe to have much fun with an empty paper towel roll any more. But put a big cardboard box in the yard, and they seem to think it's a car or a house. Or a deadly enemy. And they do still enjoy playing with rocks, sticks, and the garden hose. That's what they do when they're playing outside, so I assume it's fun. That's how I remember most of my childhood, too.

"Go outside," my mom would say, and that was the sum total of our activities for the day. If not for the summer.

We do have one outside toy. An old swing. It's just a worn piece of two-by-six board suspended by two rusty chains, and we believe it's been in our yard for more than 50 years. When we first got the house, we planned to replace it with a two-person, OSHA-approved swing set, but we're slackers. And it's grown on us.

Both our kids have learned to swing on this swing, with no strap to hold them in. They've learned to hold on tight and keep their balance. And, by all means, keep their head down if they do fall off.

They've had to learn how to cooperate, too. We only have one swing, so our son and daughter have to take turns sitting on it. And neither one of them is good yet at getting up their own momentum, so they take turns pushing each other, too. Being the pusher seems to be nearly as much fun as being the pushee, from what I can tell.

So I have to laugh when I look back at my initial inclination to install another swing so that it would be " fair." My kids, with some fighting and negotiating along the way, have made it fair. A wonderful kind of fair.

Not the kind you get when parents say, " We have to get a toy for our little boy, because we got one for our other little boy, and we have to be fair."

I've noticed only about a million times that life isn't fair. Not in that way. I wouldn't dream of setting my kids up by letting them think that life is fair in that way.

I don't even wish it were.

Life is fair enough for Belle and Joe. Sometimes they're indulged; more often they're not. They've learned to live with the fact that we have a one-person swing. And that one thing that happens all the time is other kids get toys they don't get. Oh, well, life goes on. My daughter has actually gotten to the point where she can say, "Wow, Joe, you got a new bike." She knows by now that there are times when the situation will be reversed, and when she might get the toy she wants the most.

And I'm saving an empty paper towel roll for the occasion. Just in case. ⬿

Just dip the whole thing in bronze

—3—

I was invited to a scrapbooking party once. I didn't even know what the invitation was referring to when I read, "Scrapbooking Party." When I called to RSVP, the hostess was surprised that I wasn't aware of the scrapbooking craze sweeping the nation. I told her I didn't even own a scrapbook, and she kindly explained that the point of the party was to make one.

"Oh, okay. What for?"

"Well, for your child, dummy."

I don't think she actually said "dummy" but I knew I was one, and by then I knew I was a slacker compared to other moms. But she told me that all I had to do was bring pictures of my baby. I'd be supplied with all the other materials.

"What materials?" I almost asked. But I realized I'd been enough of a dummy for one phone call, so I thanked her for the invitation and committed to giving scrapbooking a whirl.

I arrived at the scrapbooking party a little late, so the activities were well under way by the time I traipsed in. It only took a quick glance at the table where a dozen women were gathered for it to hit me; I probably shouldn't have given this particular endeavor a whirl.

The hostess had mentioned a scrapbooking craze, but didn't say they had all gone bananas. My plan for the evening had simply been to organize my snapshots and get them mounted in an album. But that doesn't even begin to describe what was going on around the table.

One woman was decorating a page with stickers, hand lettering, specially-cut borders, and funny voice bubbles around a photo of her baby boy eating from a jar of baby food.

It was, she was saying to those admiring her way with the pinking shears, his first time eating solid foods. Peas, in this case.

Hot dang! No wonder she was going all-out to commemorate this most stupendous milestone in the life of her child.

That might have sounded sarcastic, but the truth is, I felt inferior. I was way, way out of my league with this crowd. I'd thought it would be enough of an accomplishment if I could even begin to organize my daughter's baby pictures. That had been hanging over my head for the better part of a year, and I was willing to have peer pressure be the reason I got it out of the way.

But I knew I was way too much of a slacker to ever create

one of these masterpieces.

For a moment, I wondered if it would be possible to hire one of the non-slacker moms to do it for me. But then I realized I didn't really want the finished product anyway.

Because I couldn't help wondering what would happen if the little pea-eating angel ever saw that scrapbook. Don't worry, I managed to keep that to myself. But can you imagine what the boy would think if he found out how exceptional and momentous his every move was in the life of his parents? Do you think he might develop a little bit of an overblown ego? I would be worried about that, if I were the mom.

But no one besides myself seemed to be concerned, and they were all having a merry time turning each and every photo into its own little one-page shrine to whatever the occasion had been.

Since my uneasy evening in the world of scrapbooking, I've found out that this is, in every way, a craze. One that isn't merely sweeping, but has overtaken, the country. That there are entire stores given over to its pursuit, and conventions and websites where the scrapbooking devotees can gather to share the latest techniques and buy the latest patterned papers and special glue sticks.

As a matter of fact, a scrapbooking convention recently

took place in our state, and I read in the newspaper that after a given number of scrapbooking classes at a certain level you could actually be awarded a degree. In scrapbooking.

Maybe it's a great way to socialize, maybe it's fun. Maybe I just don't get it. Maybe I'm wrong when I say the content of scrapbooks is sometimes so trivial and predictable.

Or maybe I just think it takes way too much time. There, that sounds right.

In a way, that admission makes me feel even more like a lazy mom than I did before. Actually, I feel conflicted. Like two different people. I'm known as ambitious and energetic at my job, which makes me wonder why I sometimes have these slacker inclinations as a mom. I'm sure if I took my Type-A personality and applied it to scrapbooking, I could do a bang-up job.

But it's too late for me. I didn't even get a picture of Belle taking her first steps, much less eating her first peas, and there's no going back. I do have a picture of the first time she sat on a horse, but only because somebody else took it.

I guess digital technology would enable me to scan a photo of her head and insert it into pictures of other kids reaching all the expected milestones . . . but oops, that would be missing the point, wouldn't it? And just as much of a pain in the rear as the real thing.

I shouldn't pick on scrapbooking just because I flopped at it. There are lots of other expensive and time-consuming ways to make a big deal over cherry-picked moments in our kids' lives. I know a mom who takes her kids to the photo booth at a shopping mall several times a year to get their pictures taken with the Easter Bunny or the Pilgrim or the Pumpkin Head, depending on the season.

I wouldn't wait in line for Santa Claus, much less the Pilgrim.

I'm not sure why I'd want photos of my kids taken on the holidays so enthusiastically promoted by the shopping mall management anyway. Is that better than a photo taken because they had meatballs for dinner? No, it's worse, because it requires a trip to the mall.

And what would the picture tell me, looking back on it? It would say we were there. We were at the mall again. Yes, we waited in line and we got our turn, once again.

Just count that among the many things we slacker moms probably haven't done. Oh, it's just the beginning. "I was going to bronze my kid's baby shoes, but darned if I didn't lose them." Or "I forgot to write down his first word, and I'll be damned if I can remember what it was." (Slacker moms are prone to loose language.) Or how about, "I did all that stuff for my first baby, but only half of it for the second one, and now I'm doing nothing for the third."

It's enough to make you feel like you're such a lemon of a parent, you must not even love your kid.

Yet no one will come away from raising their child without some wonderful and meaningful mementos. The ones my mother kept to remind her of my brothers and me gave me some surprising insight.

I remember the day I found them.

I never thought of my mother as sentimental. She was a rancher, so she couldn't afford to be sentimental. She was a midwife every spring to a thousand mother cows, and she cared for them with a skilled and gentle hand. Nevertheless, some of those newborns died in her care, sometimes even in her arms. And her sense of pragmatism always won out over whatever feelings of sadness she may have had.

On the occasions when we lost a calf, she hauled the carcass to the "bone pile" and, from what I could tell, forgot about it, turning her attention to the animals that were still living.

My mother died in a horse accident the morning of her 61st

birthday. I had no opportunity to prepare myself for this punch in the gut. By the time I heard about it, her life had been over for two hours. I was just about to pick up the phone that morning to tell her "Happy Birthday," when instead, my brother's call came through to me with the news of her death.

It took a long time for us to come to grips with the idea that this improbable event had really happened. That she had slipped away, and from the back of a horse, at that. Not that you doubt it when somebody informs you that that's the fact, but you don't understand the scope of the situation until some time goes by. It doesn't fully register that she is never coming back. That you can't even say good-bye, much less tell her you love her. And will not have any more chances to explain, or question, or apologize.

These facts take hold a little at a time. That was part of the reason that it was more than a year before my brothers and I got around to going through her possessions to sort and distribute them.

One of my jobs was to clean out her bathroom drawers. A task left to me because I was her daughter, and these were her personal and intimate things.

The items I found in those drawers were still just as she'd left them over a year before, on that last morning when she got dressed, brushed her teeth, put on her hat, and walked to the barn to saddle her horse.

In her top bathroom drawer, as expected, I found everyday objects such as her hairbrush, toothpaste, and face moisturizer. But alongside those I found odd mementos from the lives of each of her children.

I was surprised at the nature of the objects themselves, but also because I never suspected she kept that sort of thing. Even if she did, I would've thought we'd find them in some album or special box in the storage cabinets above the washer and dryer, not in her toothpaste drawer.

There was a receipt from a jewelry store in New York, but it didn't itemize any purchases. The scrawled handwriting of my older brother, who was probably five years old at the time, was the only thing on it. " Lobe you Mary," barely legible, was all it said. (We called our parents by their first names, following the example of ranch hands.)

There was also a recipe my younger brother had submitted for a kindergarten cookbook, with directions on how his mother made shrimp, his favorite meal. " Cook until nighttime," was one of the instructions.

Then there was a " book" of poems I had written when I was

about eight. I remembered writing and illustrating it and stapling the pages together. Reading them in my mom's bathroom that day, I noted nothing beyond laborious rhymes. Fairy tales involving hay bales. Dreck. But my mother had kept this crude little project, along with scraps from the childhoods of my brothers, in a spot where she could glance at each of them every day.

I knelt there and cried as I thought about how she'd stashed these flimsy reminders of her children in her bathroom drawer. I pictured her calloused rancher's fingers touching them as she rummaged around for a pair of nail clippers.

I realized then that my pragmatic rancher of a mother was as sentimental as any mom. I know these things wouldn't have been any dearer to her if she'd been more methodical about collecting them. And I never did find among her things, even in the cabinets above the washer and dryer, any of the typical keepsakes or any kind of organized history of what we did and where we went.

I'm slightly more organized than my mom was in this regard. For one thing, I don't have a herd of cattle to minister to, so I'm not as busy. I also think I'm more of a softy than she was, in light of the fact that she didn't cry when a calf died and I can get watery-eyed over a dog food commercial.

But no one has enough time to commemorate every meaningful occasion in their child's life. Especially when you include all the things that might be defined as meaningful. That's the difficulty, I suppose.

What's meaningful in a kid's life? Every moment, potentially. But I suspect that every moment is potentially trivial, too, once we start pasting them all up.

Let's say Joe wins the Pulitzer Prize. I don't want a photo of that mounted in some album alongside the first time he hit a hockey puck. I realize that could just be my way of letting myself off the hook, as I tend to do.

Of course, if he does win the Pulitzer, I'll probably have forgotten the camera. And I'll just end up with some nonsensical scraps in my bathroom drawer for Belle and Joe to puzzle over after I'm gone.

Oh, well, at least they won't ever have to think their eating strained peas qualifies as an accomplishment in my mind.

I guess that's why fanatic record-keeping bugs me. It's not just the tedium. I'm leery of making such a big a deal out of my child's very existence, because there's a difference between real accomplishment and just being present.

I've read articles by child psychologists who have identified "lack of self-esteem" as the evil at the root of so much bad, even criminal, behavior. I don't know if that's right. But even if it is, I don't believe Belle and Joe will gain self-esteem by constantly being told they're special just for being there.

I don't think I was ever told I was special, not once. That won't come as any surprise to those who knew me as a child. But I do remember being told, "We've hired a new hay hand, if you could please teach him how to rake this afternoon."

Yes, it was true, I was the best rake driver on the place that summer. The new hand was a guy from New England who was 25 years old, and I was 14. I don't think anyone in the working world felt better about themselves than I did that day.

I was just following in my mother's tire tracks. During World War II, all the ranch hands working on my grandparents' place were called into military service. So, at the age of nine, my mother took over one of the raking jobs. When school started, the hay wasn't all in, and there was a family discussion as to whether or not she should return to school on time.

Ultimately, they decided that she would, because my grand-mother could take over her raking until school got out. But the school bus would not even come to a full stop at the ranch on those afternoons before my mother would leap off and go running for the tractor. She couldn't wait to take the steering wheel from her mother, even though she sat barely tall enough in the tractor seat to see through it.

She knew she was needed.

I'm sorry to say I don't have a tractor for Belle or Joe to drive or a raking job for them to do. But I hope they'll have that same kind of self-esteem. The kind they'll get from accomplishing a goal that isn't easy. Learning a skill that eluded them at first. Or finishing a task that really takes time and effort. Praise from others, including their parents, whom they may even want to please, is no substitute for any of the above.

Doing things just to elicit our applause won't get them very far, anyway. Our kids are still too little to be involved in team sports, but when and if Belle starts playing soccer or joins a swim team, she won't see me or my husband on the sidelines yelling our heads off. She's going to have to have a better reason for playing her hardest than that.

When I was growing up, my parents didn't do much yelling from the sidelines. For one thing, they weren't usually on the sidelines, because my parents did not even show up at most of our sports competitions. Not unless they had volunteered for some duty, such as running the starting gate in a ski race.

We went out for sports because we wanted to, not because

my parents were pushing us. And there was no point in playing to impress them once we were there. They didn't even make a big deal out of it if it turned out, afterward, that we were the star of the game.

"What game were you the star of?" my older brother Brad will ask. Fine, fine. I was never the star of any game.

I do remember, though, my mother being very proud of my younger brother Matt's performance in a junior high football game. No one can say whether or not Matt ever scored, or if his team won the game. What's important is that at some point, his friend Kevin, playing for the opposing team, had the ball. Kevin was tall and stout, older than his classmates. My brother's nick-name at the time was "Wimpy."

I'm sure Kevin outweighed Matt by at least 50 percent. But Matt tried to tackle him, jumping on his backside. Having Matt around his waist didn't even cause Kevin to drop a knee, but he was slowed some while others came to Matt's aid.

"Matt tried to tackle Kevin Larson," my mother announced to my father the minute they got home. Bragging wasn't like her, but Matt had done something that day that really did impress her.

She didn't normally make a big deal out of our failures, either, however. When I was in elementary school I performed poorly in one piano recital for no reason other than I hadn't practiced. My mother had attended this recital, but she didn't say a word about my halting rendition as we drove home in the car. She probably yakked about what we ought to make for dinner.

She didn't need to give me a review of my performance because she knew I was embarrassed and mad at myself. And she knew I could decide if it was worth it to practice next time or not without any further advice or commentary.

Her approach prepared my brothers and me to take responsibility for our own success or failure in our activities, and life in general. If we succeeded, it was because we made up our own minds to succeed, and put in the hours to succeed. It felt good when it paid off. We didn't need my parents to jump up and down over it, we were happy enough. It wasn't important whether they memorialized the events we participated in or the milestones we achieved. We'd never forget those few moments we stood on the podium.

And I will always remember the humiliating sound of quietly polite applause after a flubbed piano piece.

I hope that for my kids, too, success will be its own reward. That they'll do their best because they want to win for themselves and for their team, without even calculating my reaction, much less having it be the driving force. I don't think they'll care that I'm not always standing there on the sidelines, snapping photos of everything they do, to be pasted up in the commemorative album of their lives.

They'll have wonderful recollections without that, and so will I.

But I don't suppose that the keepsakes I end up with will come in a form that either of us could predict. My meager collection of skiing trophies seemed like a big deal to me at one point in my life, but my parents didn't have them on display. I know they cared about whether or not I skied my best, but I guess they didn't think that was always represented by the medals.

My mother was more attached to Brad's first love note. She couldn't let go, for some reason, of Matt's uncertain idea of how to cook shrimp.

And why on earth she kept my first (and last) book of poetry for 30 years, only she could know. ⇜

chapter 4

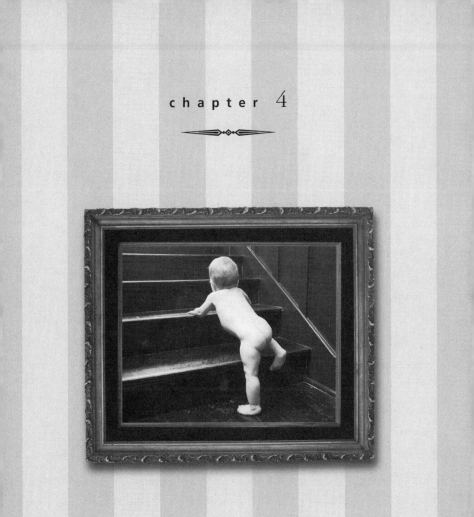

The world isn't childproof

−4−

I seem fated to let my children do a lot of things that other people have correctly pointed out could be dangerous. When Belle was a toddler, for instance, I watched her drag a chair over to the cabinets and use it to climb up on the countertop.

I realized it was possible for her to fall off and hurt herself. But at the time she had some purpose in mind − fetching a cracker, I think.

As a mom, I was impressed with her personal initiative. As a slacker mom, I was just glad she could do things like that for herself so I could sit there and continue reading the newspaper.

"Would you please get me one, too?" is probably all I had to say.

I do realize it's extremely cavalier of me to even broach the subject of child safety. I'm sure most people would say that our children's safety is a good thing in an absolute sense. And that any suggestion that we can be less diligent about it is just absurd. There's no such thing as "too safe." No mom likes to see her child get even so much as a scraped knee, isn't that right? Wouldn't I, as a mother, prevent even those if I could?

Alas, no. I'm not saying I would actually stick out my foot and trip little Belle or Joe as they ran by on the sidewalk. But I wouldn't try to prevent their taking a tumble on their own.

For one thing, it would be a round-the-clock job if I only had one child, forget two. So that's out for practical reasons alone. But I don't want to do it anyway, because I want them to find out that a scraped knee hurts. And that it's better to watch out where you're running on those uneven sidewalks.

We didn't have sidewalks on our ranch. But there were plenty of other things to put us in peril. During the summer, we were often unsupervised for most of the day. And there were horses to kick the stuffing out of us. Wild cows to run us through barbed-wire fences. A shop full of tools to inflict burns, cuts, and puncture wounds on us. And ditches so deep that your Farmall Super C tractor could actually drop out of sight if you didn't watch the road.

I'm not saying that it was a good idea to allow us as much freedom as we had to entertain ourselves in this environment. We got in plenty of trouble, and sometimes even pretty serious trouble. I wouldn't wish that on any kid or mom. But then again, along with the broken bones and stitches, there were some invaluable lessons.

I learned how to let the clutch out slo-ow-ly so my tractor wouldn't pop a wheely and go hauling over backward. My brother learned never to throw handfuls of gravel at the bulls when you're on the same side of the fence as they are. We all learned how to stay on the back of a horse when you're flying over an irrigation ditch. And that we ought to keep our balance if we were going to hang out near the hayloft window.

That hayloft one has really stayed with me.

In fact, I think I was the type to learn everything the hard way, but the lessons were indelible. Which leads me to conclude that my kids might be safer, in the long run, if they experience in the short run that the world is dangerous.

We human beings must have our own built-in safety mechanisms, otherwise none of us would survive. But it seems like those mechanisms have to be developed, kind of like our immune system.

I don't have an extremely scientific mind, but from what I understand, if one's immune system is not exposed to germs from the time one is a baby, it doesn't properly develop. We are designed not only to be exposed to germs but to actually contract illnesses from them. It's one of the most important ways we manufacture antibodies so we can fight off more serious diseases later on. I'm not trying to sound like an authority myself, I'm actually quoting our pediatrician.

That's one reason why I've never gone overboard in keeping our house free of dirt. Not lazy, then. Just trying to follow our pediatrician's advice and expose Belle and Joe to their allotment of germs. Furthermore, I haven't bought in to our culture's obsession with bodily cleanliness, and I've outright ignored the antibacterial soap fad. And, despite dire warnings to the contrary, I've let friends and relatives pass my new babies around to kiss and admire.

I do have my limits. In fact, when I looked around for Joe at the airport one time and found that he was right behind me at the top of the escalator with his tongue splayed out on the moving handrail, I snatched him up by the collar and tried to wipe off the surface of his tongue with my dirty coat sleeve.

I'm still not sure which application of germs put him further ahead on the antibody fast-track.

Just as we build our immune systems by exposure to germs, learning firsthand that we can get hurt, when we're little, must be how we develop skills and prudence. Attributes which might save us from getting into really big trouble later in life.

That's why I'm wary of going overboard to protect my children from hurtful experiences. And I'm not sure how much I appreciate some of the steps other well-meaning entities have taken to keep my kids safe from harm.

When we remodeled our kids' bathroom, the plumber who installed the valves adjusted them so that, even if you had it on full-blast hot, it was barely warm enough for a comfortable bath or shower. When I discovered that, I called and asked him to come back and readjust it so that there was at least a semblance of hot water. He explained that it was a safety issue, and that there were certain guidelines designed to protect my kids from burning themselves.

I told him that my kids, then at the ages of two and four, already understood hot water. They had been allowed to use the water faucets in the kitchen and other bathrooms. We simply pointed out to them right off which valve was hot and which valve was cold. Then we did a few trial runs of each, and they understood immediately why it was important to test the water before sticking their body parts into it.

I would be much more worried about what might happen to them if they breezed around under the assumption that all water valves in the world were temperature-controlled to prevent them from burning themselves. Because they're not.

And besides, hot running water is a good thing – just ask my grandmother – it's practically miraculous. Sometimes we need the water to be hot, sometimes we need it to be cold, and sometimes we need it to be somewhere in between. It's a modern marvel that all of that is routinely under our control.

At least, I thought it was until the plumber informed me otherwise.

If the plumber was just trying to tell me that our house had its hazards, he was right about that. My kids have gotten lots of scrapes and bumps under our own roof. I hope, of course, that they'll never sustain a really serious injury, at home or elsewhere. But in the event that they do, I think they might have a better chance of healing if it's not wholly unfamiliar territory.

One of my best friends, who was raised on a ranch in another part of Wyoming, accidentally blew his right arm off with dynamite when he was 16. He lost part of his hearing as well. But Charlie went on to live a scandalously great life. He told me that one of the reasons he not only survived his ordeal but flourished, was that he'd suffered numerous minor injuries as a consequence of ranch life before the explosion.

More important, no one had ever made too big a deal out of

them. He'd never been made to feel that he was exempted from working hard, or being cheerful, or challenging himself just because he got hurt. And Charlie never did let up on himself the rest of his life.

My mom was sad for us when we got hurt, but, like Charlie's mom, she didn't baby us. She didn't usually try to save us from our mistakes, either, even when she saw them coming.

"Sure, go ahead," I can hear her saying. "Go to school without a coat if you think that's smart." She figured I could decide for myself if I'd look cool enough that it was worth it to actually be freezing to death.

My brothers, Brad and Matt, preferred more memorable risks than going around underdressed. I remember them describing to my parents a plan they had to build a wooden rocket car with lumber from the scrap pile. They were going to equip it with wheels, so that they could take it up to the peak of the shed roof, hop in, and launch themselves down the metal roofing panels and out over the gravel yard next to the shop to see how far they could go.

They'd had a good look at the slope of the shed roof, one that was initially very steep but which flattened out about 15 feet before you came to the edge. They figured they'd go shooting out pretty level for a while before they came down for a landing.

My parents listened with raised eyebrows to this nut-brained idea but had no comment. Brad waited on the defensive to counter their objections, but didn't get any.

"So," he said with some indignation, "is that okay?"

My dad shrugged. "Sure," he said. "Have at it."

I guess this response made my brother suspicious. Or, more likely, he knew deep down that it was a pretty stupid idea. So he continued, impatiently, "Don't you think we'd get hurt?"

My father's reply: "Yes, I do."

I'm sure, on further reflection, that both Brad and Matt were capable of conjuring up a visual in which the daredevil ride concluded with a high-speed crash on the hard ground of the shop yard and a tangle of body parts, two-by-sixes and pea gravel.

The flying wooden car never materialized.

I hope it doesn't sound like my parents didn't watch out for us or take care of us. I think they were trying to teach us how to take care of ourselves. Around our place, you really did have to watch out if you were going to make it through childhood with a minimum of injuries and scars. My parents were just treating my brothers and me like we had noggins of our own.

I didn't have a very good one, frequently. I fouled up a lot, like when I sewed two zigzag stitches of black thread through the end of my thumb, at which point the needle became bogged down in my thumbnail and I, having no leverage to turn the motor, had to wait for my brother to come home and extract me from the sewing machine. By that time I was done crying about it and was able to agree with Brad that, yes, what I'd done was quite fascinating. Too bad we didn't have a camera, I nodded.

I'm not sure if I should lock away my sewing machine right now or just hope that neither Belle nor Joe is ever that big an oaf.

I'm sure some safety measures are good. I have no argument with car seats, for example. I do like to argue, though, and would argue that car seats will never approach the importance of driving defensively. I wish there were as much emphasis placed on avoiding accidents as there is on surviving them.

But as you go down the scale from car seats, you could spend your whole life and your entire savings account trying to make your environment perfectly safe for your children. And you wouldn't succeed.

Not only that, you might be left with the false impression that, having done all you can, you *are* in control of their future, and you *can* provide completely for their safety. That's something so potentially dangerous it even scares me. Because we're not in total control. Our children have more control over what happens to them than we parents ever will.

In any case, there are too many unforeseeable occurrences. Probably everyone has been to a home where the parents have taped up the entire circumference of their coffee table in bubble wrap. My parents never did that, as if you wouldn't guess. But even if they had, it wouldn't have saved my brothers' scalps.

My brother Matt got his biggest gash careening into the fireplace and landing brow-first on the grate. I doubt anybody reading this has bubble-wrapped their fireplace grate. Don't rush home and do it, though, because it will lose its mystical power to attract your kids' heads. They'll just land somewhere else. The cabinet corner. The front steps. The bathtub spout.

"If your kids don't have at least one set of stitches by the time they're seven," a fellow slacker mom told me, "you're overprotective."

I'm sure no one will ever accuse me of being overprotective, but I do warn my kids, if you fall off that fence it'll probably hurt. I might even go and grab them, but only if I think they're headed for real trouble. Because I know that if I allow my kids to experience life in a way that includes hard knocks, the type you get from pitching yourself off a fence, they'll tend to have

61

better judgment next time.

And I believe that good judgment will take them a lot further than safety measures or safety rules.

When I was working for a New York ad agency and living in Manhattan, I noticed immediately that seasoned pedestrians didn't obey traffic signals. Of course not. It is beyond stupid to step off the curb in midtown Manhattan just because the WALK sign is flashing. When you cross the street and how quickly you hustle depends on your personal judgment of how fast oncoming traffic is approaching, and whether or not they have any plans to stop. You have to make your own assessment of whether or not a particular right-turning cab driver is aware of, or even concerned with, pedestrians in the crosswalk.

Likewise, it's just a dumb waste of time to stand like a moron on the sidewalk, waiting for the WALK sign to light up if there are no cars in the street. You walk when it's safe. You wait if it isn't. This rarely coincides with what the flashing signs say to do. If I had relied on traffic signals to tell me when it was safe, rather than on my own judgment, I'd have been a statistic on about day two.

My kids are growing up in a middle-size city, not a cattle ranch and not the streets of Manhattan. They don't have to watch out for charging bulls or heedless cab drivers. But we seem to have all kinds of everyday-type mishaps handy around here to help them develop their judgment. Belle's learned not to tip her chair over backward by pushing her feet against the table. Joe's learned how to avoid tilting his trike over and dumping himself elbow-first onto the concrete driveway. Those are just a few of the mundane calamities that I, slacker mom that I am, stood by and let happen.

I've noticed that giving them my opinion on the matter is generally not enough to convince them anyway. But their personal experience is more than enough. I don't think I've ever seen them make a mistake twice.

I think they're taking away something even more valuable than the lessons about specific dangers, too. That's the notion that, as much as their parents love them, we can't always be there to protect them. And that they'd better watch out for themselves.

But I do wonder if a lot of adults were at some point led to believe that someone else was supposed to be watching out for them. That if they've suffered an injury, or even illness, it must have been because of a fundamental breakdown in "the system," that someone should be held responsible for. In court, preferably. I always want to ask them what system they mean. The solar system? What system is supposed to protect us from ever being hurt?

Then again, I'm not sure I can blame people for feeling victimized. I must admit, I felt that way when my mother died.

My mother, that day, should have been safe. Riding was something she did almost by instinct. She was probably in top form that day.

It was her birthday, so she could have decided to be taken to a sumptuous breakfast, to be treated to a massage, or just to sleep in. Instead she chose to get up early and work. To see the sun rise from the old comfort of her worn saddle. But midmorning, her horse shied frantically and reared over backwards so fast that she didn't have time to throw herself out of the way.

Granddad and Brad were shortly contacted by the sheriff and told that she'd been in an accident, and they got to the hospital in time to meet the ambulance coming in. They were expecting to find out if she'd sustained any serious injuries, but instead were informed by the ambulance driver that she was already dead. A little bit later they were led into a room to look at her body, and to lift the sheet to see for themselves that she'd died with her boots on.

My brother told me about how he and Granddad left the

hospital together. Brad walked silently to the car, too devastated to say anything. Granddad, heartbroken over having just lost his only daughter, had a comment I wouldn't have predicted.

"Well," he said, "we're all mortal."

When Brad repeated this story and Granddad's remark to me, he added that it had provided him with some comfort, which I didn't comprehend. It sounded like an odd response to what I knew was the worst turn of events in my grandfather's 84 years.

I felt bitterly wronged, myself.

But as the days went by following her memorial service, I thought more about the phrase "we're all mortal" and it began to take on a significance which has provided comfort to me ever since.

65

What Granddad so generously meant, and Brad more readily understood, was that vulnerability to death is a condition that's shared equally and fairly by all of us – by everyone who is living. Even his beloved daughter was subject to it. It's the very essence of being alive, and is not confined to the elderly, or the sick, or even to those who are doing something dangerous.

My mom's death, then, wasn't unfair. It was just a miserable manifestation of the fact that the world is not safe or predictable.

That realization has made me feel less victimized, and, along with the sheer passage of time, is the thing that's most helped me stop feeling sorry for myself.

In any case, her death didn't make the rest of us feel that we shouldn't ride. In fact, the day after her memorial service, my brothers and I, along with other family members and friends, were out on horses at four in the morning, gathering up the herd of yearlings she'd been in the process of moving onto their summer range.

As the sun flickered over the meadow at dawn and lit across the backs of the trailing cattle, I rode with my feet in the stirrups of my mother's saddle and felt sure that we were right where she would have wanted us to be.

Right here in this wonderful, unsafe world. On horseback.

It still hurts, though. Sometimes that makes me want to protect Belle and Joe from emotional injury, even more than physical injury. Because I know that heartache can be worse than a broken bone. And last longer. Yet, it's essential to their happiness that they're able to take emotional risks. Because not taking them would mean Joe wouldn't run for class president because he might not win. Or Belle wouldn't try out for the basketball team because she might be relegated to the bench. Or Joe wouldn't ask a girl out on a date because he might be turned down.

I know their emotional pain might leave a scar, but I also know it might be fortifying. When my grandfather was in grade school, he had a debilitating stutter. He happened to be walking past the bunkhouse windows one day, when he overheard a few of the ranch hands laughing about his halting efforts to form words and sentences.

The ranch hands, "meaning no harm," according to my grandfather, were imitating him, joking that he'd probably do quite well, that he'd probably be "g-g-governor one day."

I'm sure my grandfather was shamed and hurt, but he was also indignant.

"By God, I will be governor someday," he said to himself.

He eventually overcame his stutter with the help of a speech clinic and his own tenacious will. And in 1962, Granddad was elected governor of Wyoming. He went from there to the U.S. Senate, and remained in public service until he finally "retired" to cattle ranching. He is a riveting speaker to this day.

Our own three-year-old son, Joe, was born with a neurological impairment called nystagmus. It's an inability to control his eye muscles that hasn't slowed him down so far. But it looks strange to other people, and probably means he's in for some teasing. I'm not looking forward to this, but I'm not too worried, either.

67

From what I know of my son, he reminds me of my grandfather.

Maybe emotional blows are like physical blows. You stand to gain something if you sustain them from time to time. You might build up some inner strength you wouldn't otherwise have.

Both my grandfather and my one-armed friend Charlie took some pretty deep wounds in life. Visible and invisible, ones I wouldn't ever want my children or yours to have to bear.

But when I think of them I find I'm simply impressed by what people can overcome. ⤳

chapter 5

There goes Harvard

–5–

I was once asked to write a recommendation for the son of a friend who was trying to get accepted into an exclusive institution of learning. I'd known him all his life, so that should have been pretty easy to do. You would think I'd have some idea of what to say, so the school would be able to make a fair assessment of this person's chances of succeeding in its environment.

But I was stumped, because the applicant in question was two years old.

"He's never thrown up on me," I began. "And he doesn't scream at an excruciatingly high pitch like my own two-year-old."

That's when I almost called this preschool to ask them if they'd ever heard of drawing straws. I didn't understand how they could select and reject applicants based on a system of merit. I would think all the two-year-olds had equally runny noses.

Criminy, as my mother used to say. Yet, from what I've heard, this is nothing compared to the preschool competition in bigger cities than ours, where kids are put onto waiting lists before they're even carried to term. I can only assume these schools care more about a parent's ability to write checks than a kid's ability to group objects into sets.

I also know that education is a topic of great concern to everyone – not just the parents who have kids in the school system. I'm sure some people believe the very future of our society lies in the hands of our schools.

Plus, we're spending a boat-load of money on them, so of course we're interested in whether or not the schools are doing a good job.

In fact, the school board elections in the small town I grew up in were often more hotly contested than the state gubernatorial race. It was something to get elected. My dad got elected to the school board one time, and I don't remember his being puffed up about it, but I was.

" My father's on the *skoo-ul* board," I reminded my friends to make it sound like I actually knew something about the institution of junior high. And I went along for quite awhile thinking about how certain teachers better not continue to cross me because it just might cost them their jobs.

I was disabused of that notion the first time I complained

to my dad about one of them in particular – the prim home economics teacher who gave me a "D" in sewing.

"Maybe it was because your pants only had one leg hole," he suggested. He placed no blame on her punctilious teaching style or the fact that she expected me to pay rapt attention in class.

I admit, having a father who was once on a small-town school board is about the limit of my pertinent expertise. I didn't major in Early Childhood Education. I'm not a teacher. I'm not an educational psychologist.

I don't know how to "fix" public schools or raise our national test scores in geography. I don't even know if either of those is necessary. The only thing I remember that needed fixing was the lunch menu.

I'm just speaking to the new moms who might be, as I was, taken aback at the pressure on their kids to get into the best school and to excel in academics at a very early age.

I didn't spend much time evaluating preschools to figure out the best one for my daughter. I was ambivalent about sending her to preschool in the first place because I didn't start school until kindergarten myself. And, not to brag or anything, but I won the county spelling bee.

In any case, I had several friends who'd practically prepared

Excel spreadsheets on the relative advantages and disadvantages of every preschool we knew of, so as the slacker mom, I could mooch off them. It seemed like all the schools had their merits. As well as their shortcomings.

And I suspected my daughter's success would have less to do with our choice of schools than it would have to do with her work habits. Which aren't just developed at school; they're developed at home, doing mountains upon mountains of laundry.

Oh, wait – those are my work habits, not Belle's.

I ended up choosing her preschool partly based on the fact that it was the closest one to our house and would cause me the least amount of inconvenience when dropping her off and picking her up. I'm a busy person, what with all the laundry.

It's not that I don't care about her education. I do. But I can't be convinced, especially at her age, that it's important for her to be the first one to read. Or do equations. Or identify lots of different kinds of dinosaurs.

A lot of other moms I know seem to be concerned about this and are, in my opinion, unduly delighted with their children's progress in these areas. I'm secretly annoyed by that kind of precocious learning in the case of five-year-olds.

So, that's a stegosaurus? An herbivore, you say? Did you

know that you're standing on my foot?

I read that Aristotle believed children should not be taught to read until they're ten. That, until then, they should focus on music and exercise. Whoo-boy, that really appeals to my slacker mentality.

But I realize a lot of people, including my own husband, would be upset, if I didn't let Belle and Joe learn to read until they were ten. I might even be put in the slammer.

Maybe they'd be right. Maybe today's children mature much earlier from an intellectual standpoint. But I think Aristotle's point is still valid. That knowing how to read is of limited value until you understand the content of what you're reading.

It's like being able to recite "two plus two equals four" without having a clue about the mathematical principles involved. It seems more important that a young child's brain learns to make sense of mathematical ideas from objects found in the natural world.

Marshmallows, for instance. (I realize, if you've read the label on a marshmallow bag you could argue with me about my definition of "natural.")

I didn't come up with this revolutionary teaching method, though. My children did. If Belle has one marshmallow, and Joe has three, she can see that she needs to filch one of his, pronto.

From a math standpoint she might be quite the little prodigy, now that I think of it, because she figured that out really quickly. Then again, maybe she's just greedy.

In fact, as far as social and friendship skills go, she still needs more work to understand all the reasons you don't go and grab somebody else's marshmallow. And good manners are so much more important than math, at any age.

Food and mathematics seem to coincide frequently in our household. For one thing, Belle and Joe are very keen judges of quantity and mass when it comes to what's on someone else's dessert plate. And, if you really want to be impressed with my home-schooling techniques, here's what happens when we make that dessert ourselves.

First, look at the picture on the back of the cake box. (It's disheartening, I know, that we're not making this from scratch.) What does the recipe say? Three eggs? Get them, please. Carefully. Oh, the butter needs to be softened. Will you put it on a plate and put it in the microwave? Press the "1." You can stir it, Joe, but keep the spoon on the bottom of the bowl so the batter doesn't go flipping out.

Belle, do you remember where the measuring cups are? We

need the middle-sized one, and we need it full of cold water. Not hot, cold. Oh, should we make cupcakes instead, Joe? It is "cupcake," not "pupcake," by the way. Get the pan, please. Do you think we'll need to make more than one batch of cupcakes to use up all this batter? I think so, too. Let's see how many we have when we're all done.

Belle and Joe don't seem to realize that cooking can be a most tedious chore. And that so can math. They actually think they're having fun, the little sweethearts, while they learn to cook, to count, and to judge volume and spatial relationships. As they watch the cupcakes rise through the oven window, perhaps they're even getting some vague idea about the tendency of heat to expand things. (Not that it will stop my cupcakes from ultimately cratering in the middle anyway.)

They're also learning how rewarding it is to use that knowledge and those acquired skills to some desired outcome. In their estimation, the outcome doesn't get any better than chocolate cupcakes.

Happily, I'm relieved of the burden of contriving some artificial system of gold stars to try and make them feel that they've done well because they said their ABCs. Maybe when they get older, this association with practical ends will translate into laying their own brick patio instead of going to the gym to lift dumbbells up and down.

I'm not saying schools should now replace academic subjects with Cupcakes, Bed Making and Laundry Sorting. I just question the value of isolated math, science and literary skills – especially when they're achieved at the expense of social skills – when our kids are little. I don't see how it's putting them ahead if they know how to write their name before the next kid.

I see how it puts us all ahead, however, if they can make their own sandwich before the next kid. Or clean up their own messes. Or feed their own pets. In fact, the sooner Belle and Joe can fend for themselves by doing tasks such as those, the better.

I realize that puts me in danger of becoming even more of a slacker as a mom, but it's a risk I'm willing to take. On behalf of my children.

My own father, Pete, expected us to fend for ourselves, but he didn't push us to excel in academics. Of course, it would have been pretty hypocritical if he had. Pete was a high school dropout himself. A fact he might not have mentioned in his school board campaign literature. Oh, well, too late now.

I know it's difficult to read the word "dropout" without

making a judgment about the person, but I assure you my father is smart, and what most people consider to be very successful. He just doesn't have much formal education.

When my dad was nine, his father was killed in a boating accident, leaving him and his older sister, Andrea, to be raised by their mother. That wouldn't have necessarily derailed their education, except for the fact that at the time, my grandmother wasn't exactly focused on their schooling. She was focused on skiing. She'd been captain of the Eastern Women's Ski Team, and owned and operated a ski resort where they lived in Vermont.

Both my father and Andrea were fast skiers, but compared to the other women, Andrea was more than fast. She flew. She was named to the U.S. Ski Team when she was barely a teenager. At that time, the ski racing that counted was taking place in Europe. So she bid high school adieu, and commenced a grueling tour of European ski resorts, honing her turns to the point where she eventually won two gold medals in the Olympic Games. Oslo, 1952.

Maybe my aunt set the precedent. Maybe her success was part of the reason my dad's mother wasn't paying any attention to what was going on in his life. Either way, he dropped out of school, too, and never went back.

He joined the National Guard when he was 17, fibbing that he was 18. When he came home from the war in Korea, he got into the ski business, then the cattle business, and then the real estate business. I guess nobody ever thought to ask him for his diploma.

Nonetheless he's been an inspiration to my brothers and to me. To work hard, ski fast, and not get too fixated on formulaic methods of success. We children had our own reasons for staying in school, anyway. In fact, I'm the only one of us who doesn't have a graduate degree.

Even if Belle and Joe are like we were and stay in school, and even if they, unlike us, get straight A's, I wouldn't assume they're headed for future glory.

I do know a boy and girl who've benefited from their parents' high regard for academic achievement. But they've suffered from it, too. They are several grades ahead in reading and math skills, but don't try to throw them a ball because it'll bonk them on the head before they can catch it.

The poor kids are embarrassed at this. Who wouldn't be? And it's humiliating, always being the last ones chosen for teams. It's hampered their social skills and left them ill-prepared to operate as team players later in their lives. That's a real deprivation because there are so many great teams to play on in life. A family, a business, a marriage, a community.

It's not just that they can't do such things as catching balls, though. They're not even familiar with the concept of unstructured play. When asked to play outside, they don't want to go. When booted outside anyway, they have nothing to do and hang out on the porch until they're allowed back in.

The ability to play, and have fun, and even learn things without being given an earful of instructions must come naturally to kids. Because even babies can do it. But it must also be something they can forget, once they get used to having everything structured. So that, if told nothing more than to "Go out and play," they wouldn't know what to do.

My slacker approach to motherhood happens to dovetail nicely with the concept of unstructured time. I feel fine about placing the onus on my kids to figure out something interesting to do.

Of course, when I say "interesting," I don't mean changing clothes in the car as we speed from music lessons to soccer practice, from dance recitals to play rehearsals, from basketball games to birthday parties. As far as I'm concerned that's deadly dull, not interesting.

Taken one at a time, all of these activities, no doubt, have merit. I do think it would be fine for Belle to learn ballet. I whole-heartedly endorse the idea of Joe's learning to play an instrument. I would love it if they both embraced the sport of skiing. But being able to entertain themselves and figure out what to do with their own time are skills that outrank any of those.

That's one reason I plan to be extremely choosy about the activities I allow on our calendar. The other reason, I confess, is that I don't want to be the shuttle driver.

I already have a job, thank you, and I actually get paid money for it. I want to have the time to pursue it and do well at it. And I don't think that's a disservice to my kids.

81

I'll never forget listening to some relatives discussing the outcome of a lawsuit that my sister-in-law had successfully defended on behalf of her client. My eight-year-old nephew was there, too, but I didn't realize that he was paying attention to this relatively dry conversation until he added this remark to the discussion: "My mom sure is a good lawyer."

I was impressed that he was impressed, at his age, by his mother's abilities in her profession. I bet this is part of what inspires him to do well in school, and he does do well. She's not pushing him to succeed, she's pulling him. Because she's setting that example and she's someone he genuinely admires.

Thank goodness for me that I, too, had parents who inspired me rather than pressured me. I would have collapsed under the weight of knowing that any little slip up, curricular or extracurricular, would cause my parents to sigh, "There goes Harvard."

Or, more likely, I would have utterly rebelled. And it would have been, "There goes sixth grade."

My parents didn't expect us to be superkids. They expected us to be independent. A kid probably can't be both. To be a superkid, you've got to constantly have parents, club leaders, coaches, and instructors telling you what to do, when to do it, and how. You won't be able to think for yourself, or come up with something to occupy your time, or figure out how to go about it.

My brothers and I grew up thinking for ourselves. Even though that sometimes led to stupid mistakes, especially in my case. My mom and dad didn't have the time or the inclination to always be telling us what to do or how. If my parents gave us any instructions at all, they usually amounted to, "Don't spare yourself and you'll do fine."

That's about all my mom told my brother when she handed him control of her business and livelihood.

82

My mom ran for governor several years before her death. Her friendly, outspoken charm and lifelong leadership in numer-ous endeavors outside the realm of ranching had made her both well known and liked throughout the State of Wyoming. And she succeeded in winning the primary election and securing the nomination of her party. She and my father were divorced by then, so she was running the cow business single-handedly.

Before my mother set out on her ultimately unsuccessful attempt to unseat our then-governor in the general election, she installed my younger brother, Matt, on the ranch to keep things going for her while she traveled to every community in our state.

Wyoming elections, then as now, are won on doorsteps and in high school auditoriums. Not on radio or TV.

My mom didn't have much in the way of instructions for my brother, as she entrusted him with a 2,000-cow operation. But she did tell him one thing.

"When you're gathering up the cattle," she said, "you've got to ride the outside fence line. You'll ride harder and longer than anyone else, but it's the only way you can make sure you're not leaving a single animal behind."

With that, she left for Cheyenne.

I hope Belle and Joe will do well in their endeavors.

83

Including school. But it'll be their choice, and their way. For my part, I can't think of any better instructions for them than what my mom said to Matt.

Ride the outside fence line, kids.

Ride the outside fence line.

chapter 6

A bathroom of one's own

-6-

I'm sure you'd never do anything so idiotic as to pack and move your household, including your one-year-old baby, when you're eight months pregnant, six days before Christmas, on your husband's birthday, in a wet snowstorm.

And I would never do anything so idiotic a second time.

Not that I planned it that way the first time. We bought our old house in a state of long-established neglect and disrepair, and we realized we'd have to fix it up quite a bit before we could move in. We calculated with keen and careful prudence that the overhaul would take six months. Seven at the outside. Which would have put our move date comfortably in the middle part of summer.

It was an excellent plan.

At that point, anyone with any intelligence could have told us to take our best, most conservative estimate of the construction timeframe, and double it. Putting our move date squarely in the latter part of December. At a time when I'd be begging someone, anyone, to induce me into labor.

That doubling formula works equally well for the budget, incidentally.

But none of the improvements we made seemed to be optional. In order to park in the narrow 1920s garage, we would have had to buy ourselves Model-Ts. The kitchen was newer, but my pot holders and dish towels really didn't coordinate with the avocado-green appliances – which still worked just fine, amazingly. But I'm sure that color won't be fashionable again until about, uh . . . 2005 . . . oh, crap.

The most serious deficiency, though, was that the house did not have, had never had, a master bathroom.

87

Fortunately, there was an old sleeping porch next to our bedroom, which we magically – just by writing out checks – transformed into a lovely master bath. Not only did we want this new bathroom for ourselves, but we also thought our kids should have the existing bathroom just for themselves.

As we designed the new bathroom, it seemed like a sensible, if not mandatory, improvement. Especially in the event we would ever have to sell the place.

It was hard for us to imagine how the home's prior occu-pants got along without it, frankly. Only two other families before ours have lived in our house in the three-quarters of a century it has been standing. The kids of both these families were born and raised there, somehow shepherded through all phases from infancy to adulthood under that roof. Coincidentally, both of these families had eight children.

One bathroom. Eight children. Is there a better definition of hell on earth? When we first went through the house, I remember how that gave me a cold shudder. How could they live like that? And remain on speaking terms?

But now I've thought about it more. And I realize that life in our household, with just the four of us, is more likely to generate feuds. We can actually afford some measure of chaos, lack of discipline, and selfish behavior, but when you have to parcel out time in the bathroom among ten family members, you can't. Instead, you'd have to learn early on, almost from infancy I would think, how to get along with each other and work around each other.

Not only did the families before us have to share (and be extremely disciplined about limiting) time in the bathroom, but they must've been on top of each other when they weren't waiting for the shower, too. This is not a large house I'm talking about. Average families didn't build enormous houses in the '20s the way they do now. The kids were doubled or tripled up in the bedrooms, and probably had to eat breakfast in shifts.

But think what skills they had to learn in order to make it unscathed through the morning, not to mention high school. They had to be able to plan, to cooperate, to quickly resolve disputes. Imagine if, when finished in that one bathroom, a kid left his dirty pajamas on the floor, and toothpaste globs in the sink. Minor offenses, perhaps, but multiply them by ten and you can see how everybody would want to be more courteous. Although I'm sure these family members had to learn compromise and forgiveness, too.

All of these are such valuable skills. Ones that, no doubt, served these kids well once they left the household. So maybe our house was a great family home just the way it was, before we made it "livable."

But I've heard many couples say their goal as parents is to give their kids more than they had. Their own bedroom, or bathroom, or just stuff in general.

I don't have this goal. It's easy to write that off to the fact that I'm an admitted slacker. I'm not a slacker at everything, though. Just as a mom. I actually work overly hard at my job, but not to provide my kids with more personal space or stuff than I had, which wasn't a lot of stuff compared to my friends. My parents

89

deprived my brothers and me in an ingenious manner, and I can only hope to do the same for my kids.

Actually, I don't think my parents or the parents who occupied our house before us were trying to be ingenious. They probably just didn't have the extra money. If you do have the extra money or a willingness to go into debt, it's tempting to want to provide your kids with lots of their own space and lots of their own stuff. But as they get older, I can see how it might take my kids someplace I really don't want them to go.

A place where they each have their own room, of course. They each have their own bathroom. They'll each need their own TV in their own room, too, so they don't have to watch anybody else's show.

Keep up, now. They must each have their own computer. Otherwise they can't do their homework because sharing makes it horribly inconvenient. And, if they're going to have any kind of social life, they've each got to have their own car, so they can come and go without the bother of coordinating schedules with anyone else. They can't talk to their friends, not really, if they don't each have their own phone and their own number to go along with it. And speaking of privacy, they'll each need their own credit card so they don't have to ask me to buy something for them and then have me wreck their plans by saying, "No."

It might sound like I'm exaggerating, but I think I've just described life with teenagers in the average American suburb. And it's an easy trap to fall into. I've gone down that road and my kids aren't even old enough to have any of the items I just talked about. It starts earlier than that, I can testify.

I don't know what your child's adorable first word was. "Mama," perhaps, or, "Dada." I'm pretty sure Belle's first word was "mine."

And you have to understand what Belle meant when she said, for instance, "my cup." It did not mean just the one she happened to be drinking out of right then. No, her cup meant a cup that was purchased for her and her alone. It had Snow White on it, by God, and no one else was allowed to sully it. Specifically, not her little brother.

At first, I didn't see that as a big problem. I didn't really understand where this "get your hands off that" idea could take us. I thought I was just being a fun mom when I bought my kids their own plastic plates, cups, bowls and even spoons and forks with popular television characters that, for the most part, are gender-specific. Leaving no doubt about which item belongs to whom. It's not like bikes for two different-sized kids, which would have a functional difference. It's about control. I got about ten plates, twenty utensils, and a dozen drinking cups into this before I realized where it was leading, and that I'd rather have a paper cut.

One place it was leading, by the way, was to individualized meals to go along with the personalized place settings. Have you ever found yourself making one thing for the adults for dinner, one thing for one kid, and another thing for another kid? Did that make you feel like you were the bestest mom in the world, or, like me, did you stop and wonder if you'd accidentally handed out menus at the beginning of the meal? If you'd somehow done something to communicate that the people you were cooking for should have a choice of entrees?

That's not the outlook I want my kids to have, where everything is customized for them and things have to be done their way.

I can see how that could turn them into a real pain in the neck for all the waiters in restaurants, a hazard to every other driver on our crowded freeways, and the worst possible kind of tourist in any foreign country.

So I've finally ridded my cupboards of all those one-person items, and we've managed to create a more communal, family-oriented existence. One where my kids eat what's been prepared for the family, or don't eat. And where we have a shelf full of drinking cups, and you use the one that's in front. It's only yours for as long as you need it, and then it gets cleaned and put back on the shelf for the next person.

At first, this seemed so marvelous that I thought I'd invented this amazing system, and wanted to patent it. But then I realized that it was just normal.

But let's talk about something more substantial than Bob The Builder cereal bowls. Because it is easy to assume your child will be a bigger success in school, and their future career, if you buy them their very own, say . . . personal computer.

Maybe. Maybe not.

I read about a woman who was hired to head up a large and embattled division of a telecommunications conglomerate. According to the magazine article, the fact that her company faced a bigger, more established, and better-funded competitor didn't phase her. Because growing up in modest surroundings outside Pittsburgh, she competed with five siblings for "food, clothing and shelter," as she somewhat jokingly put it. Then she put herself through college and law school with jobs at McDonald's, a garment warehouse, and a tractor factory.

After reading about this woman, I asked myself which

93

might tend to give my daughter the skills to succeed. Having her own computer or having to use the family computer on which three other people demand their own time? Perhaps I'll have my daughter just share the one computer.

Wow, maybe I'm not a total slacker as a mom after all. I'm increasing Belle's odds of becoming the scrappy head of some come-from-behind company.

"Thanks, Mom," I can hear her saying in the not-too-distant future, "for not letting me have any of the things I ever wanted!"

Actually, that doesn't sound like the Belle I know and love.

But I do hope that both Joe and she will be good at sharing the world they live in. That they'll know how to politely negotiate their way through a busy, crowded parking lot. That they'll be able to stand patiently in a ticket line waiting their turn behind a bunch of strangers who might have obscene tattoos or body odor. That they'll have the personal mettle to sit and respond politely to interminably bad service at some chain restaurant.

These aren't heroic accomplishments. They're just social skills.

My grandparents have impeccable social skills. Maybe that's just the way they are. But I don't think those skills are genetic or I presume I would have inherited more of them. It might have had something to do with their circumstances.

When my grandmother married my grandfather and moved onto the ranch, it was the end of September in 1934. Coming into winter in that part of the world. The cow business was tough even in good years, but then the country was in a depression. And every dollar left over after paying the help and buying supplies went to the land and cattle fund. My grandparents couldn't afford to build a house for themselves, so they moved into the bunkhouse with the ranch hands. And they lived there for the next six years.

It was close quarters for this bride and her new husband, and for the baby girl and boy that came along shortly. Four hired men were quartered there with their bedrolls and few possessions in the back room and on the second floor of this simple log building. My grandparents lived downstairs so my grandmother could be closer to the kitchen, where she cooked the meals for herself, Granddad, and the help.

When asked about bunking with the ranch hands, she simply says, "They were all nice men."

If my grandparents hadn't been extremely well-mannered before the bunkhouse years, they would have been afterward. To this day my grandfather will say, "Excuse me, Martha," if he has some inkling that he is standing where she might want to walk.

The words "after you," and "please forgive me," and "no hurry" come readily to both of them.

My grandparents treat everyone deferentially. Employees. Store clerks. Even telemarketers. They never seem to be thinking, "Oh, I'll never see you again."

But most impressive is the way they treat each other.

I'm sure that my grandparents' excellent manners toward each other are one reason they have an interesting, fun, and romantic relationship after nearly 70 years of marriage. And who wouldn't want to live with someone who had such good manners? I don't mean how to properly set the dinner table or address heads of state. Although my grandparents know both of these. I mean how to treat the people around you with respect, compassion, forgiveness, and humor. Even your own family members.

I know that, in our times, my grandparents' situation in the bunkhouse is an extreme example. One I'm glad I don't have to follow – I've been through potty-training with indoor plumbing and I'm really not sure how it works in the winter with an outhouse. And I also realize people can be brought up to be well-mannered even if they live in a large house.

But I still believe the more space and stuff our kids possess that's exclusively theirs, the fewer opportunities they'll have to learn skills of sharing, planning, patience, and problem-solving in what is, after all, a communal world. So when I heard some friends say they wanted to have another baby but were prohibited because they didn't have another bedroom, I couldn't help but offer "Let the kids double up" as an alternative. I could tell by the look on my friends' faces that they were wondering how they got so lucky as to be given the benefit of my free advice.

At least they were nice enough not to point out that, like so much advice, it's not followed by the giver. Belle and Joe each have their own small room in our old house. I hope, in spite of that, that they'll still have some of the social skills possessed by the 16 kids in the two families who lived there before us. They were both great families and raised wonderful children from what I know.

One day, 18 members of the family who'd resided in our house in the '30s, '40s, and '50s rang our doorbell. I'd just gotten home from my office, had no idea if the beds were made, and didn't feel like entertaining large groups.

But when I opened the door they announced that they were having a family reunion, and asked if there was any possible way they could have a look around the old house they grew up in.

"Hell, no!" I said. "And next time, how about picking up the phone and giving me a call first?" Then I slammed the door.

Actually, that's not what happened. That's just what flashed through my mind before I managed to smile widely and say, "Absolutely! Come right in!"

My husband and I spent the next hour with them, and it was a hoot. They had a scandalous story for every room of the house. These siblings were still good friends, their husbands and wives now included.

We learned that there'd been a conflagration in Joe's room, when one of the boys gathered up the girls' hair ribbons and made a campfire out of them in the closet. It explained why his doors and woodwork don't match anything else in the house. We heard about how they flew down the banister and nearly out the front door, what types of items got hardest stuck in the laundry chute, and how easily my kids would be able to sneak out in the middle of the night.

Other than the sneaking out part, this is what I wish for Belle and Joe. That they'll still be friends 60 years from now. That they'll have fantastic stories from growing up in our old house. And that they might ring its doorbell someday with their spouses in tow.

Having called first, of course. ⇜

chapter 7

Don't make me mad

-7-

As a slacker mom, I am very fond of "natural consequences" when it comes to punishment. If Joe decides to eat a family pack of Cheetos, I think vomiting is a fit penalty. My jumping up and getting mad, and doling out my own form of punishment, would simply be redundant.

So I can just stay right where I am with my lovely cup of tea. Aaah.

My mother certainly didn't overwork herself in that regard. Right before my fifth-grade pictures were taken, I decided to give myself a makeover, and I trimmed up the bangs and sides of my curly hair with my dad's shaving razor. When I'd finished creating my new look, I resembled a poodle.

Do you think my mom got mad at me? No, she just sat there and looked at me for a moment, then turned back to her book in an effort not to laugh loudly.

Not only did she not scold me, she didn't run me over to the beauty salon in town to see if anything could be salvaged. The slacker. But I didn't need a lecture from her to wish like hell I hadn't done that two days before they took my class photo.

I'm really glad I found out how this system works when I was little. I'm grateful that my parents didn't "protect" me from it. I've tried to follow their lead and let the natural consequences make themselves known to my own kids whenever possible, usually just by staying out of the way.

But we parents don't really want our children to suffer the natural consequences of, say, running out into traffic. So, as they skittle heedlessly toward the curb, we might find ourselves screaming something ironic such as, "Stop right there before I kill you!" And then looking around to see if any of the neighbors heard us because we wouldn't want anyone to think we would ever lose our temper and yell.

They might decide we're rotten parents. Out of control and probably ineffective, too.

But as my neighbors can tell you, I get mad at my kids. And I holler at them. I also say things I regret on occasion. I try to make sure I apologize, but I didn't stop being emotional or fallible when I gave birth. Besides, I don't think getting mad is necessarily ineffective.

It works pretty well on a car trip, anyway. My husband was

off somewhere else one time, and I was driving Belle and Joe to my dad's place for the weekend. Two hours into it they started provoking each other with an efficiency that can only be achieved by blood relations. Grabbing the bag of pretzels and wagging it just out of reach. Then kicking, hitting, and hair pulling. Followed by screeching and screaming.

At each of these violations of good manners, I told them, over my shoulder, to stop. "Belle, share the snacks with Joe." And, "Joe, don't kick your sister." And, real loudly, "Quiet!"

But my kids knew that my attention really had to remain focused on the road, and nothing I had to say slowed the escalation of the conflict.

Finally, I'd had it with the screaming and crying, along with the kicks on the back of my seat. I pulled the car off the road, which was a big surprise to them, and came to an abrupt stop. They were already silenced by this troubling turn of events. But they were even more alarmed when I turned and spanked both of them sharply on their thighs (I couldn't reach their behinds), and yelled that if they didn't stop fighting in the car, we would turn right around and go home!

"Right after hell freezes over," added the more rational part of my brain.

My kids were smart enough to know I wouldn't make good on that threat, too. We were 120 miles up the road. I'm aware that parenting books say that's the Number One Disciplinary No-No, making threats that you can't or won't follow through on.

But the empty threat didn't diminish the impact of my words or actions one iota, because the feasibility of carrying out my promise was not the point.

The point was, I was spitting mad. I was mad enough to pull off the road and stop the car. Mad enough to haul off and whack them, and then yell at them with a wild-eyed look on my face. They didn't like it at all, that I was that mad, and after whimpering for a few minutes, they behaved like model citizens for the next hundred miles.

I think Belle and Joe understood when I pulled the car off the road that one of the consequences of bad behavior is that it tends to make other people irate. So even if you don't have a better reason to be good, you'd better not be too bad or you might really tick somebody off.

I know, child psychologists might tell us we've completely missed the target if our children behave only because they fear our reaction. And most times, they're probably right. Because so often, in the case of bad conduct, there is a natural consequence we can let our children suffer for themselves, so they take away a memorable and meaningful reason to be good.

But a lot of times there isn't one, and we have to impose our own consequences. Time-outs, for instance, which I'm all for. Time-outs work well for our kids because as soon as they're made to leave the room they believe the rest of us immediately start eating candy and watching cartoons.

Time-outs also set a logical precedent since isolation from others, right up to a stint in the federal penitentiary, is what intolerable behavior usually leads to.

Time-outs are not a "natural consequence" though, because they require the intervention of parents, if not law enforcement. Otherwise, you'd get away with your antisocial actions.

Just like you'd get away with screaming at and fighting with your sibling when you're traveling in the car. Someone has to intervene because there aren't any other consequences. You could keep it up for hours! You're both buckled in your car seats, so you're really not going to hurt each other. You're just going to drive all the other passengers, not to mention the driver, right up the wall.

And you can't exactly be strapped onto the luggage rack for a ten-mile time-out. Though I must admit, I enjoyed the few minutes I contemplated that.

Looking back at myself as a kid, I know that I was afraid of what my parents might do if I acted that way. Damned afraid. I didn't like to see them mad, for one thing, but for another it stung to be swatted with a wooden spoon. My parents seemed to become more reasonable as I got older, or maybe I gradually gained some understanding of the rationale behind the household rules. But I knew the rules had to be followed way before I thought they had any merit.

Partly because they spanked me when I willfully misbehaved, especially if I was disrespectful on top of it. I know it's asking for trouble to advocate spanking. It's like plastic surgery. The minute you say it has some merit, there are just some people who will go and take it too far.

The thing I remember about a swat on the behind, though, is that it left no room for interpretation. You didn't think, "I wonder if she means that I should continue to stick out my tongue at her when she asks me to clean my room?"

My, how efficient it would be if your kids understood, from the outset, that when you said not to do something, you meant it. Think of the trauma and trouble it would save you both down the road.

You'd never have to get sucked into that predictable downward spiral, where their behavior, and your reaction to it, just gets worse bit by bit, until you're finally saying, "I've told you 68,000 times not to do that!" And then asking yourself why your kids apparently didn't believe you when you said it the first time.

Little kids are not unlike horses, I guess. For one thing, it's easier to catch them if you can get them to come to you rather than chasing them all over the pasture. More to the point, I know from growing up riding horses how difficult it is to have any control over them if you've waffled in the beginning about whether they're going to go where you want them to go or wherever they please.

A horse will often settle this issue as soon as the rider's in the saddle. Or even before – by smartly walking off when we're just throwing a leg over. At this moment, we should pull back on the reins to say, "When I'm ready, thank you." But if we're inexperienced riders (or parents), we just laugh nervously and say, "Oh, well, here we go!"

We don't think there are any dire consequences to letting the horse (or child) dictate to us. What the heck, we were planning on heading out of that very same gate ourselves.

But there quickly comes another time for the horse to find

out who's in charge. At a creek crossing, for instance. The horse might think, "Slippery rocks, cold water . . . not today." So he balks. But nay, we insist! We give a little kick and point the horse right down the creek bank again. The horse, however, sensed back at the barn that we were not entirely sure if we were in control. So the horse may toss his head and hop back and forth a little.

Now that he's put up some real resistance, of course, it's the worst possible time for us to capitulate. Because if we do, we're essentially telling him, "If I give you any trouble, just give it right back, and then some!"

When I think about parenting issues in terms of horses, it all seems so clear. So straightforward. But when dealing with your own small children, it's easy to hedge, isn't it? I admit, I've reenacted the creek-crossing scene many a time.

I don't have to tell Joe, "You be the horse and I'll be the milk-toast rider." Joe and I both know our parts.

Here's me: "No, you may not have candy before dinner . . . well, just one." Or: "No, you may not sleep in our bed . . . well, promise not to kick." Or: "No, you may not watch any more TV . . . well, turn it down." It's all the same, just a slight variation in script and scenery.

I hope when Belle and Joe are old enough to read this, by the way, that they'll have spent a lot of time around horses and that they'll be flattered rather than offended by being compared to them.

I saw another poor parent play the role of the hapless rider in a toy store one time. As they stood in the checkout line, the little boy kept telling his dad he wanted a certain airplane.

"No," the dad said, "we're here to buy a birthday present for your sister and that's all." So, as all the other parents tried not to notice, the kid started throwing a fit, hopping up and down.

Like a horse, come to think of it. I guess I didn't try hard enough not to notice.

The dad was embarrassed at this, but even more so when the kid bleated, "You never get anything for me! You get everything for Megan!"

I was wishing at that moment that the dad would sit up in the saddle and show us all how it's done. Would escort the kid out of the store, explaining that not only will he not buy him the airplane, but he won't even allow the kid in the store if he's going to act like that. And then drive him home.

But the dad didn't. He instead said authoritatively, "Well,

okay, but this is an early Christmas present."

Still in charge, then.

I could certainly sympathize with him, and I'm sure all the other parents in the toy store could, too. For one thing, who wants to drive your kid all the way back home without accomplishing the errand that brought you to the store in the first place?

That would be highly inconvenient.

I once read a convincing article by a mom who said indeed, that's the reason so many kids are not disciplined. It's inconvenient.

She described how when their kids were in junior high, they'd paid what was for them a lot of money to take the whole family to an amusement park for the day. But just two minutes after they got inside the gate, the kids started fighting with each other verbally and physically. So the mom and dad took them each by their elbow and marched them out of there and drove them home.

Wow – those expensive tickets, and an entire day of family fun, down the drain. Just to let their kids know they wouldn't allow that kind of conduct. How inconvenient is that?

"Excuse me?" you might be thinking, "You – the slacker mom – are now suggesting we do something that's inconvenient?"

That may seem like an abrupt departure, because I've been saying all along that we can all put our feet up and relax, right? That parenting needn't be so much trouble.

But I stick to my guns. Because, I ask, which is more inconvenient? Walking out of an amusement park, toy store, movie, or whatever just once (I bet that's all it would take), or facing the same kind of bad behavior every time we take our kids somewhere, dealing with it in the same feeble, ineffective way, time after time?

There you go. I'm putting my feet up on the sofa right now.

Speaking of feeble and ineffective, I had to laugh when a friend of mine told me about a parenting class she took and the New-Age-y advice they were dispensing, including that a parent should never use the word "no." They did furnish some watered-down euphemisms for "no" such as, "That's not okay! That's not okay!"

But among other things, my friend wondered how she was supposed to protect her children from hearing the word "no" once they left the house for the first time. She's noticed that it's a rather popular little word.

My own children know how popular it is. They've discovered that other people besides myself get mad, and don't hesitate to use the word "no."

At our community pool one day, Joe did not obey when the lifeguard blew the whistle and announced it was time for the hourly ten-minute break. I was already out of the water with Belle, and I saw from my chaise lounge that Joe was not getting out, disobeying an order he understood full well and had always minded in the past.

The lifeguard didn't blow her whistle again. She didn't yell out her order again.

She knew Joe, and she knew that he'd heard her perfectly well the first time and was blithely ignoring her. So she got down from her perch to crouch in the shallow end of the pool, nose-to-nose with Joe, and told him if he didn't obey the rules and do what the lifeguard said, he wouldn't be allowed to come back to the pool ever again. So, *out. Now.*

Ride 'em, cowgirl. I hope this lifeguard becomes a mom someday. Or owns horses. Or takes over that inane parenting class.

Joe was already halfway out by the time she finished her persuasive little speech. He was mortified that someone besides his mom had to get mad at him in front of everyone there. He'd discovered he could get into trouble with someone other than his parents.

The consequences of his misbehavior at the pool were swift, sure and unequivocal. If not purely natural – that would have been leaving him in the water to drown. Instead he was bawled out by the lifeguard. Just like when he makes somebody mad at home.

I went over and thanked her for doing what I should have done.

But sometimes stern words from good old mom don't do the trick as well as stern words from a lifeguard.

My husband and I took a two-week vacation when the kids were very small, while one of my single friends moved in to take care of Belle, Joe, and the dogs.

When we got back, I found that my daughter's vocabulary had acquired some off-color inventory. Most disagreeably, the word "shit." She wasn't being bad. The word had been absorbed into her growing repertoire like any other, and she used it in the proper context.

It was jarring, though, to hear a two-year-old say, "Shit, my cocoa's hot."

I got right on top of the situation. "Belle, don't say 'shit' any more," I commanded.

"Why, Mama?"

"It's a bad word."

"Why is it a bad word?" she asked.

"Umm . . . because it means 'poop'."

"Is poop bad?"

"No," I wobbled ahead, "poop isn't bad. But there are just some words that are rude and that's one of them. So don't say it, and I mean it."

"Okay, Mama," she said. "I won't say it any more."

You must admit, I'd cleared that up quite handily. I'd taught myself a good lesson, too, because I now realized that as long as I articulated to the children which behaviors were unacceptable and why, they would cheerfully comply. No more spankings, that's for sure!

"Mama, I won't say 'shit' any more," announced Belle the next day, out of the blue. "I won't say shit, and I'm not going to say shit."

Blast, she'd outwitted me. She had put the word into the one context where I was stymied as to what to say. What I really felt like doing was laughing. But I sensed that would lose me strategic and moral ground, so I left the room.

After a few minutes, I got my head together and marched

back in there.

"Belle," I said, "if you say that one more time, I'm going to give you a spanking."

Thankfully she knew me well enough that I didn't have to. ↩

chapter 8

———◆———

Now all you need is a village

-8-

During one phase of my career, I flew 94 segments on one airline during one calendar year. I remember because I'd come painfully close to reaching the most elite passenger status with this airline, one that would have secured my seat in first class for the following 12 months.

I was traveling so much, I had almost no home or social life at all. At the same time, I wasn't traveling enough, being six segments short of having my servile existence made a little cushier by wide seat cushions and free cocktails on every flight.

It was one of those bad news/bad news situations. I've never liked those.

This phase of manic business travel continued for a while even after I came back from the maternity leave I took with Belle. I am married to the kind of guy who is a full partner and doesn't have to be nagged to a frazzle to pitch in and make sure everyone's taken care of. But he had his own job to go to every day. So, in addition to having the contribution of a spouse who's a wonderful father to our children, I hired a full-time nanny.

I know. Having hired help as I raise my children is enough to send me straight to Dr. Laura Hell.

But it's been said that it takes "a village" to raise a child. And I say, hire one if you have to. Neither my husband nor I have any relatives nearby, so in our case, "village" means "nanny, babysitter, daycare, or play group."

We know there may not be anyone in this world who loves our children as much as we do, but we've discovered there are lots of people who can provide Belle and Joe with loving, and even exceptional, care.

I was raised in a village myself, in a manner of speaking. Almost all the employees who worked on my family's ranch resided there, too. And some of them with their own families and children. I'm sure it's partly because I profited from growing up around so many people – and different kinds of people – that I felt good about having help to care for Belle and Joe.

I remember just about every person who came through our place, and I think they each added something important to my understanding of the world.

My parents' criteria was an honest ability and a willingness to work, without much regard to personal traits.

So quite a variety of people were hired over the years, although some of them were not people you'd put at the tippy-top of your baby-sitting list.

I remember more than once my father being notified by the sheriff of a ranch hand drying out from some bender at the county jail.

But one of those who often smelled of whiskey rescued me from a runaway horse when I was four or five years old. I was scared enough to scream loudly, and naturally I got the opposite reaction I wanted from a poor horse who was probably more terrified than I was. This ranch hand raced to my rescue, grabbing the reins of my bridle just before we proceeded through the barbed-wire fence at a dead run.

I will always remember another crewcut employee who chewed tobacco and used swear words and who I thought for sure was a man, but my brother said was really a woman.

What mattered to my parents was that this person could dig post holes and pitch hay. Ranch work goes on seven days a week, most of the year. And it usually involves physical labor. So a lot of people wouldn't be interested in it or good at it. But she was.

I say "she" because I think my brother was right about her

physical gender, and once I began to suspect that, I admired her more than ever.

My parents knew the ranch operation stood to benefit from the contribution of all different kinds of people and personalities. But we all benefited. I can't imagine having grown up without Ray, our loyal irrigator for 60 years, or brothers Marty and Wayne, the world's best mowers when sober, or Margaret, the loopy cook who married Wayne.

And I will never forget the tragic Garcia. He was one of my favorites, partly because he always spent some of his earnings on candy for my brothers and me. But one day my father told us we wouldn't be seeing Garcia any more.

"Garcia is a good man," is how my father began. "But he killed another man in a knife fight. Although it was self-defense, he's going to prison."

We never saw him again, but I always imagined that he was thinking about us, locked in his cell. I believe he cared about my brothers and me.

I often wish Belle and Joe were growing up on a ranch. I don't suppose any of the caregivers they've had so far has ever dug post holes or strung barbed-wire, and I admit I'm including myself when I say that.

Even so, I've watched as our kids have been broadened by the care and insight they've received from numerous people of both genders, from countries such as Mexico and the Philippines, including nannies, daycare teachers, and babysitters.

Belle knows more Spanish than I do. Joe's become more confident and friendlier. They're both fonder of spicy foods than most of their peers and know how to use chop sticks.

Still, I realize a lot of moms feel guilty about all the times they're not home with their children. And I know what it's like to drop my kids off at a daycare facility that, some days, looks more like a loony bin. But when I think back on my own childhood, I'm reminded that Belle and Joe have an opportunity to pick up something really valuable, or just interesting, from each person they get to know.

Beyond that, my job is important to me. I've wanted to be a writer ever since I was in junior high school, and becoming a mom didn't change that. I'm grateful for the opportunities my career has given me to solve problems and to work with people I learn from. Almost every workday, I feel I've been given an opportunity that I wouldn't want to have missed.

So as I sort through my priorities, my children's well-being is near the top, but so is my own. Which includes my career.

Besides, I don't think my kids and my career have to cancel each other out. I believe Belle and Joe gain something from having a mom who takes care of herself, rather than one who is guilt-ridden or unfulfilled because she doesn't think she's allowed to do what she loves to do. So I have no misgivings about seeing to my own needs and pursuing my own dreams.

That's what my parents did. That's what they raised me to do. And that's the example I hope I'm setting for my kids so they'll do it, too.

Pursuing your dreams probably means something different to you than it does to me. I sure as hell hope so, anyway. I'd hate to think you'd spent as much time as I have writing phrases such as, "See store for details."

For some people I know, career fulfillment means working part-time. And I know that for some parents it means not working outside their home at all. For many, it's some interesting combination.

For the part-time nanny we have now, pursuing her dreams actually includes taking care of other people's children. Thank goodness for that.

I hear a lot of people argue that what we need, with reference to career and family, is "balance." In fact, a friend of mine, noting that my life appeared to be disorganized and patternless, gave me a package of two one-hour cassette tapes on how to balance my work and home life. Of course, I haven't listened to the tapes, partly because I'm sure they'd be boring as all get-out. But it's also because I don't believe that there is some perfect, balanced formula. When I look around at all the moms I admire, they're compromising and juggling all the time, and continually reinventing the rules as job or home circumstances change.

I think they're setting a great example for their kids by doing so. Because the kids will have to juggle and compromise, and reinvent the rules, all the way through their lives, too. Even if they don't become parents.

But while I'm juggling my children and clients, let me mention that other ball I have in the air. My dear husband. I've already said that my career is an important priority, but even more so is my marriage. I think it stands to benefit Belle and Joe if I try to set a good example by succeeding at both.

This is not always easy, of course. My clients can be a pain in the neck, but then I remember that they're paying me, and it helps. I'm doing the laundry, however, for free. And there are days when I find myself ready to clobber my husband with the egg-encrusted frying pan he left in the sink for "somebody" to wash. I'm not his mother, for Pete's sake, and I've got enough to do. But then I think back to the last time I mowed the lawn, and realize it was never.

Our relationship isn't perfect, but we try hard. We keep at it. My husband has a quick sense of humor and that's most often what saves us from going too far south. At least my kids know that two people can disagree vehemently, and still be in love. And that sometimes people (such as their mother) can even behave quite badly, and yet be forgiven.

My husband and I don't hesitate to show Belle and Joe that we care about each other, and not just about them. We hire a babysitter from time to time without any plans other than doing something alone. We even hug and kiss in front of the kids rather than bonking each other with frying pans.

We know that, by watching us, Belle and Joe are picking up clues about how people should relate to each other. We hope we're helping them set high expectations about how they themselves deserve to be treated in a relationship.

By the same reasoning, I have to think a mom is helping set her kids' expectations high for their lives by doing whatever it is that rewards and energizes her in her own life.

I know several moms who, like myself, had children late in

their 30s, and for some of them, that baby is practically a miracle child. They called upon everything that science and the gods had to offer to get their baby. When they're finally blessed with one, it seems like they feel they're being disloyal to that effort if they don't make the child the center of the world. Often that means quitting a career they've loved.

I wish I could describe to them the pride my nephews have in their mom's law career and what an inspiration she is to them. She argues facts to a jury one day and vaccinates calves the next. I sometimes wish she had a daughter, too, because I can only imagine the good a growing girl would get from being reared in this household, with two parents who love and respect each other, and who are both hard workers creating their own success according to their own criteria.

It's a lot like the household I was raised in. It's true that I never saw my father rolling out pie crust and my mother wasn't usually the one with the blow torch, but they were equals in the amount of authority they had and in the amount of work for which they were responsible. For one thing, there were too many chores to contend with, season after season, to let unfounded notions about which gender was capable of what get in the way.

My parents worked on our ranch, which was also our home. I guess I was lucky because they didn't go away to work in the morning to some office that was off-limits to kids. On the other hand, they didn't get off at five o'clock. Ranch work was so integrated into our lives that I didn't even think of it as "work." It was just stuff that needed doing, even if it happened to be Saturday.

But I never felt neglected because my parents always had work to do. And I don't feel I was abused because some of my earliest memories are of chores. I'm grateful to my parents because they ingrained in me a love of work and a habit of working. Although I now know that they weren't trying to mold me.

"We really needed your help," my father says. I remember how good it felt to be valuable, even though I was just a kid.

I did have one creative director, while rejecting me for a job as a copywriter at his advertising agency, inform me that I might want to take the entry "Tractor Driver" off my list of Previous Employment Experiences. It wasn't helping me get hired on in corporate America, he explained in the nicest way he could.

I'd been naive, it seemed. I'd thought that companies – even ad agencies – must be looking, first and foremost, for responsible people who weren't afraid to work. And tractor driving was not, as you would've gathered from my resume, merely driving. It was raking cut hay into precise parallel rows. And maintaining the levels of fuel, oil, and coolant that kept your tractor in good working order. Along with a daily greasing of all the tractor and rake joints.

But I figured this creative director represented other potential employers, so I followed his advice.

I suppose I was buying into the conventional wisdom that tractor driving is a low-end job. But now I don't think he was correct. Every job has moments of glory, but every job – tractor driving, advertising, being President of the United States – involves a lot of drudgery.

I think my experience with tractor driving and other ranch chores has made me a better employee, even if my bosses and clients can't appreciate that fact since tractor driving is no longer on my resume.

I'm not above drudgery, that's for sure.

My chosen profession is far from the hayfields of home, but it's never felt burdensome to me to get out of bed and go to work in the morning. The truth is I've always been secretly embarrassed that I often don't roll into my office until nine o'clock or later – having wasted half the morning by my own family's standards. But I've adjusted my work habits in other ways, too. I've learned to operate a computer about as well as I once operated a tractor. And I've learned to feel satisfied with the results of my efforts, even when they're something as insignificant and fleeting as a 30-second television commercial.

One time I did reach a point in my career that felt dull and repetitive. My job seemed more low-end to me than tractor driving ever had. I told my mom I was ready to quit because I wasn't doing something important. I guess it felt too easy right then, and I had started to think about how trivial advertising really was, and how creating magazine ads and TV commercials wasn't doing anything to make the world a better place.

No doubt a lot of people would add, "You're right, it's making it a worse place."

I'm not sure if my mom would have agreed with that, but I know she didn't personally relate to my career. I was downtown with her once when a bus drove by with a big ad on the side that I'd worked on.

I pointed out to her that I'd written that particular piece of creative genius, and she said, "You wrote it? It's three words."

So when I complained years later that my job wasn't important, you might think she'd have agreed. But she told me I was wrong. She said there was nothing more important than working hard at whatever it was I chose to do and doing my best at it. That there was no better way to improve the world around me.

I'm going to tell Belle and Joe the same thing, and I hope my son and daughter will experience all that's wonderful about having a demanding and challenging career in a field that interests them. I especially want my daughter to have a mother who's in the throes of that for a role model when she looks at me. I want my son to have that outlook on women so that he might choose for his partner someone who is his equal, not his handmaiden.

I realize that if it all works out as I hope for Belle and Joe, it means that my precious grandchildren – when and if I'm lucky enough to be a grandmother – will be partly raised by some kind of hired help.

Stone-cold sober, of course.

chapter 9

Has anyone seen my instinct?

–9–

If you think I should be stopped, you're not the first person. But why would I stop now? Why would I make this my last chapter when I've barely even begun to cover the topic of parenting? There are so many significant subjects I could still tackle.

Nutrition . . . Bedtime . . . Wardrobes . . .

Yes, there's so much more to childhood and to parenting than what I've talked about so far.

But I don't think I need to cover any of those subjects. Because so many other people have already hashed through them, to alarming excess. I think the surplus of information is actually more frightening than the surplus of toys, scrapbooks, and one-person cereal bowls.

Just log on to Google.com sometime and see. Did you know that a Google search of the phrase "parenting advice" produces more than a million matches?

Even if you narrow it down, you'll be submerged in

information. The phrase "potty training," for example, produces more than 200,000 matches. And several of them are for websites whose sole subject is potty training. Just think about it – that makes potty training an actual career choice for some people. And apparently they think they can make money, creating entire websites to explain a feat that human beings have been performing successfully since the Romans invented plumbing.

So I hope by now you're wondering, "How much more information do I really need?"

Maybe not all that much. Not if you're one of those funda-mentally decent persons, the parent who loves their kid. I remember the first time I was pregnant, loving my baby helplessly even though my lips had never touched her soft little cheeks. I remember seeing her face for the first time, and weeping with happiness, gratitude, and awe.

These feelings of love are surely the ultimate in parenting equipment, even though we come by them at absolutely no cost to ourselves. That must mean we're prewired to do the right thing. And that maybe we'll all do a perfectly fine job of raising our kids if we just let ourselves. If we listen to our own inner promptings.

I admit, sometimes my inner promptings are wrong. Sometimes, at a gut level, I want to tie Belle and Joe to their chairs for the afternoon. But something inside me always over-rules those urges. Maybe I'm just barely smart enough to know that wouldn't work. Maybe, deep down, I'm just about as smart as the two-toed sloth, who knows instinctively how to raise its babies without ever once perusing the parenting section of the bookstore.

And not only am I that smart, but my kids seem to be even smarter. The last thing I want to do is undermine them by underestimating them.

I know parents who speak in the third person to their kids, saying, "Mommy has to take a shower now," because they read that little kids don't understand pronouns. Kids don't understand sarcasm, either, according to the experts, but that doesn't explain why three-year-old Joe said, "Good job!" when I flipped his pancake onto the floor.

And kids aren't supposed to be able to sort out the meaning of a whack on the bottom after they've beaned their brother with their lunch box. But mine can.

Why is that? Maybe it's because I'm so woefully uninformed about their limited capacities that I expect them to understand all those things, instead of expecting them not to. In fact, I've rarely been disappointed when I've put my bets on Belle and Joe. They usually perform best when I try to keep out of their way.

I wonder if we're giving our children the chance to really perform, if we're giving them and ourselves enough credit, as we pore over our parenting magazines and reference manuals. I wonder if we're getting in the way rather than out of the way, as we get sucked into the trap of competing with other parents to raise the most exceptional child.

And I wonder if we're listening to the sage ghosts of our ancestors who did, so often, know just what they were doing as they brought a new generation of human beings into the world.

They somehow managed, from what I can tell by looking back one and two generations in my own family. That's how I know that so much of the stuff we're supposed to buy and do as parents these days is really not necessary. That even if you have none of the advantages – no exclusive preschool, no educational toys, and a complete lack of private coaching in mathematics – it doesn't stop you from being a successful person. Or even a great person.

Look back a generation or two in your own family, and I'm

sure you'll see parents who raised happy, productive human beings without a neurotic fixation on the methodology.

Mothers of an earlier generation had it easier in a way. Because the glut of child-rearing news articles, books, and equipment that we modern-day moms have to contend with is truly dizzying, even for the most clear-headed of us.

The biggest problem isn't the confusion, though, it's the seduction. We'd just love to believe that someone's discovered a secret formula that will give our children and us a guarantee of success.

It reminds me of my determination to lose weight after giving birth to Belle. Searching for the latest information on how to do it, I went online and to the bookstore. Talk about dizzying. There are thousands of books in the English language on dieting and weight loss, not counting the cookbooks. And a lot of them are "new" or "breakthrough." Buying into any of them was deluding myself, though, and I knew it. But it didn't stop me.

I wanted someone to tell me how, even though it was no big mystery. Even though I knew that, dash it all, I was still functioning pretty much the same way I always had.

The simple fact was if I ate too much, I gained weight.

I probably already know a lot of simple facts about being

a mom, too. Even if an excess of information on parenting sometimes distracts me from them. I'm probably capable of figuring things out for myself.

I hope so, because I'm not much for following directions.

I realize that, to some people, figuring out for themselves how to be a parent sounds difficult. I'm a slacker mom, so I know just how they feel about things that are difficult. But I can honestly say that, so far, following my own instincts rather than caving in to the current cultural norms has been easier, not harder. It's been less time-consuming, not more. It's cost less money, too. Oh, well, I can live with that.

But even if I did think there was a book that had all the answers, I'd be wrong. I've seen some reference manuals on parenting that make War and Peace look like a quick read, but they don't have all the answers. Partly because ideas on child-rearing change all the time.

For instance, we've been hearing for years that our kids get way too much sun – you'd have to be a two-toed sloth not to know that. But I just read an article that said today's kids are seriously deficient in vitamin-D. One reason? Not enough sun.

Didn't someone say "All things in moderation," a really long time ago? It still makes sense to me. And it's just one of the many

135

solid ideas that have been around since a long time before www.geniusbabies.com even came along.

Yes, that's a real web address, and I'm sure there are those who haven't agreed with a word I've said and are probably jotting it down. I hope they have a lot of free time and disposable income.

It's possible they'll find something useful. No doubt modern science has made more than one or two discoveries during the past decades that have added some insight to the way we raise our offspring or that even corrected the misguided notions of an earlier generation as they tried to do their best by their kids.

And, of course, they've come up with a few tools that make the job easier. My great-grandmother could detect a fever in her children by holding the back of her hand to their forehead. My own mom used a mercury thermometer. I have a digital one.

This is progress, if not from a health standpoint then at least from a technical one. And I'm a fan of progress.

But log on to the Internet sometime or go to the parenting section of the bookstore, and see for yourself the breadth and depth of detailed (and, so often, contradictory) instructions that are provided to parents of our era.

And then ask yourself: How, oh bloody how, did our parents and their parents and all the parents who came before them get along without this whopping slew of data?

Then go to one of those baby department stores and repeat the question. Just substitute "whopping slew of stuff."

Were our ancestors just slackers? Not at the time. Maybe that's what makes me one; maybe I was born 30 years too late. But maybe I wasn't. Maybe, like my parents and grandparents, I can trust myself to be a mom without a reference library to tell me how. Maybe I don't need magazines, television or the Internet to tell me how. And maybe most of all I don't need marketing campaigns designed to make money off my good intentions to tell me how.

Maybe I know how.

Or, by God, I'll figure it out. ✎